THE MOUNTAIN BIKER'S GUIDE
TO SOUTHERN CALIFORNIA

Dennis Coello's America by Mountain Bike Series

THE MOUNTAIN BIKER'S GUIDE TO SOUTHERN CALIFORNIA

Dennis Coello's America by Mountain Bike Series

Laurie and Chris Leman

Foreword and Introduction
by Dennis Coello, Series Editor

MENASHA
RIDGE
PRESS

FALCON
PRESS

Library of Congress Cataloging-in-Publication Data
Leman, Laurie.
   The mountain biker's guide to Southern California / Laurie
and Christopher Leman : foreword and introduction by
Dennis Coello. — 1st ed.
     p.   cm.
     — (Dennis Coello's America by mountain bike series)
     ISBN 1-56044-197-6
     1. All terrain cycling—California, Southern—Guidebooks.
2. California, Southern—Guidebooks.   I. Leman, Christopher.
II. Title.   III. Series: America by mountain bike series.
GV1045.5.C22S684   1993
796.6'4'097949—dc20   93-8622
                                                        CIP

Photos by the authors unless otherwise credited
Maps by Tim Krasnansky
Cover photo by Dennis Coello

Menasha Ridge Press
3169 Cahaba Heights Road
Birmingham, Alabama 35243

Falcon Press
P. O. Box 1718
Helena, Montana 59624

Table of Contents

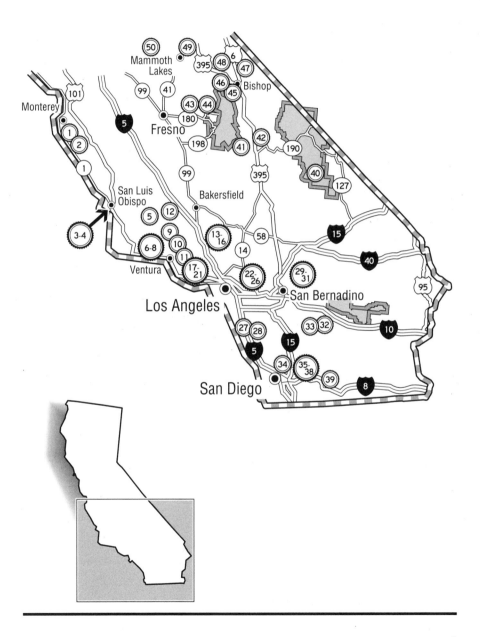

List of Maps

AMERICA BY MOUNTAIN BIKE   *MAP LEGEND*

Ride trailhead   -🚲→   Steep grade

Primary
bike trail

Direction
of travel

(arrows point
downhill)

Optional
bike trail

Other
trail

Hiking
trail

10 EXIT 382

Interstate
highways
(with exit no.)

(395)

U.S.
routes

(49)

California
state routes

Covell Blvd.

Other
paved roads

Unpaved,
gravel or
dirt roads
(may be 4WD only)

726

U.S. Forest
Service roads

Fresno ◉
Riverside

Cities

Lone Pine ◉
Carmel

Towns or
settlements

Dam   River,
stream
or canal

Lake

0   1/2   1

MILES

*Approximate
scale in miles*

N

True North

TOPANGA
ST. PK.

Parklands

*International
Border*

*State
Border*

✈ Airport

♥ Archeological
site or ruins

.) Archery range

▲ Campground (CG)

≡ Cattle guard

♦ Cemetery
or gravesite

♦ Church

⌇ Cliff, escarpment
or outcropping

⚑ Drinking water

⌇ Fire tower
or lookout

⊞ Food

⊟ Gate

♦ House or cabin

▭ Lodging

❊ Mountain or butte

❦ Mountain pass

△ Mountain summit
3312 (elevation in feet)

⚘ Military test site

✕ Mine

⚏ Museum

⚒ Observatory

♦ Park office or
ranger station

⊼ Picnic area

♦ Port of Entry

⟋ Power line
or pipeline

♞ Ranch or stable

⚖ Swimming Area

⫴ Transmission towers

⊐⊏ Tunnel

Foreword

Welcome to *America by Mountain Bike,* a twenty-book series designed to provide all-terrain bikers with the information necessary to find and ride the very best trails everywhere in the mainland United States. Whether you're new to the sport and don't know where to pedal, or an experienced mountain biker who wants to learn the classic trails in another region, this series is for you. Drop a few bucks for the book, spend an hour with the detailed maps and route descriptions, and you're prepared for the finest in off-road cycling.

My role as editor of this series was simple: First, find a mountain biker who knows the area and loves to ride. Second, ask that person to spend a year researching the most popular and very best rides around. And third, have that rider describe each trail in terms of difficulty, scenery, condition, elevation change, and all other categories of information which are important to trail riders. "Pretend you've just completed a ride and met up with fellow mountain bikers at the trailhead," I told each author. "Imagine their questions, be clear in your answers."

As I said, the *editorial* process—that of sending out riders and reading the submitted chapters—is a snap. But the work involved in finding, riding, and writing about each trail is enormous. In some instances our authors' tasks are made easier by the information contributed by local bike shops or cycling clubs, or even by the writers of local "where-to" guides. Our sincere thanks goes to all who have helped.

All of the rides in this guide have been pedaled by our authors themselves, then compared with dozens of other routes to determine if they qualify as "classic"— that area's best in scenery and cycling fun. If you've ever had the experience of pioneering a route from outdated topographic maps, or entering a bike shop to request information from local riders who would much prefer to keep their favorite trails secret, or know how it is to double- and triple-check data to be positive your trail info is correct, then you have an idea of how each of our authors has labored to bring about these books. You and I, and all the mountain bikers of America, are the richer for their efforts.

Dennis Coello
Salt Lake City

P.S. You'll get more out of this book if you take a moment to read the next few pages explaining the "Trail Description Outline." Newcomers to mountain biking might want to spend a minute as well with the Glossary, so that terms like *hardpack, single-track,* and *windfall* won't throw you when you come across them in the text. "Topographic Maps" will help you understand a biker's need for topos, and tell you where to find them. And the section titled "Land-Use Controversy" might help us all enjoy the trails a little more. Finally, though this is a "where-to," not a "how-to" guide, those of you who have not traveled the backcountry might find "Hitting the Trail" of particular value. All the best.

Preface

Southern California—it brings to mind images of blue skies, sunshine, and people enjoying the outdoors. For mountain bikers, Southern California is a gigantic playground. It is unmatched in its variety of scenery and terrain. You may be musing on a mountain lake's reflection of a snowcapped peak one day, then cycling to an abandoned mine through a painted desert the next. From riding on gentle trails along seaside bluffs, to huffing and puffing up mountain roads to view giant redwoods, this place has it all.

When offered the chance to write a mountain bike guide to this region we jumped at the opportunity. What could be more fun than researching some of the finest riding in the world? Our northern boundary begins at the Pacific Ocean near Big Sur, then crosses the state and veers north to follow the edge of the Sierras to Mammoth Lakes. The rides are located all over Southern California. There are several in the Greater Los Angeles area, and many more in national forests, state parks, and recreation areas scattered throughout the region.

With help from bike shops, forest rangers, fellow cyclists, and with regional guidebooks in hand, we honed in on some of the best rides around. The trips presented in this book are just the tip of the iceberg, a preface to the many miles of fine cycling that adventurous mountain bikers will discover on their own.

Mountain biking is great fun and tremendous exercise. Whether you are in excellent physical shape or in need of some conditioning, you will find rides in this guide that are suited to your abilities. Many of the more demanding rides in the book include suggestions for easier options.

Every attempt has been made to portray accurately the difficulty of each ride. Keep in mind that "difficulty" is a subjective matter. Some cyclists will find our descriptions to be overly cautious, while others will find them understated. We suggest that you start with an easier ride, especially if your fitness level is low or if your bike handling skills could use some work. This will give you a feeling for our rating scale and provide you with a setting in which to strengthen your riding abilities.

SAFETY, COURTESY, AND RESPONSIBILITY

Be completely self-sufficient. Be prepared to find your own way if you get lost. Use all available maps. Information is often inaccurate on maps; check their data, and make comparisons. Take note of landmarks and keep track of where you are and where you have come from. Stop often and look behind you; it may be necessary to turn around and retrace your path. Tell someone where you plan to

A grand view of the Monarch Divide.

go, your route of travel, and your anticipated time of return. Tell them what to do if you do not return by the specified time. Ride with others who may be able to provide help in an emergency, especially in remote areas. Learn first aid and how to deal with altitude sickness, hypothermia, dehydration, heat stroke, snake and tick bites, and other ailments and injuries that might befall backcountry users. Carry a good first-aid and repair kit. Keep your bicycle in good working order and know how to make basic roadside repairs (like how to fix a flat). Develop a checklist of what to take with you when riding. Wear a helmet and cycling gloves.

Ride within your limitations. Turn around if the weather becomes threatening or if you find the ride more difficult than you had expected. Keep your speed under control at all times. Play it safe on narrow roads and when approaching blind corners; someone may be coming from the other direction. Be especially careful when riding on paved roads and busier forest roads; stay to the right and ride defensively and predictably. Lower your seat and your center of gravity before beginning a steep descent. Avoid backcountry rides during hunting seasons.

As relative newcomers, mountain bikers should make an extra effort to be courteous and to ride safely. Announce your presence when approaching other trail users from behind. Be mindful of the special needs of equestrians. Horses have poor eyesight, are easily spooked, and can cause serious injuries when startled. If you meet horses on the trail, dismount and move well off the trail to the downhill side. Take up a position where the horse will have a clear view of you. If you come upon equestrians from behind, stop well in back of them. Do not attempt to pass until you have announced your presence and asked for permission. Then pass quietly on the downhill side of the horse. Give these animals a wide berth, for they are likely to kick out at you.

Be prepared for extreme riding conditions in the mountains and in the desert. Your body requires at least three days to become accustomed to high elevations. If you experience dizziness, nausea, headaches, or shortness of breath, descend to a lower altitude to allow time for recovery. Weather conditions can change rapidly; carry raingear, warm gloves, and other protective clothing to change into if necessary. Dress in layers so you can adjust your clothing to fit any number of riding conditions. Ultraviolet radiation from the sun is more intense as you climb higher; wear protective sunglasses and apply sunscreen with an SPF of 15 or better. Reapply sunscreen frequently. Lower air humidity and loss of water through heightened respiration can cause rapid dehydration at higher elevations. Carry water from a safe source and bring much more than you expect to need. Force yourself to drink even if you are not thirsty, especially on hot days. You should drink often enough to require frequent urination and your urine should run clear. Darkening of your urine indicates that you are not taking in enough water. Once you become dehydrated, you will not be able to rehydrate

The wide open spaces of Southern California.

and continue cycling. Carry high-energy foods and eat often; drink water with your snacks and meals.

Respect the environment you are riding through.   Bicycles are not permitted in Wilderness Areas or on the Pacific Crest Trail. Some public lands restrict bicycle use to designated trails and roads only. Obey all signs indicating road or trail closings. Never trespass on private property. Always stay on trails and roads; cross-country riding is inappropriate and often illegal. Never travel on worn trails where cycling will cause further damage. Carry your bike over degraded sections of trail to reduce further damage, or turn around and return the way you came. Do not shortcut switchbacks or ride around waterbars placed in the trail; help control erosion instead of creating further degradation. It is never appropriate to skid your tires, even when descending tight switchbacks. If you cannot control your speed without skidding, dismount and walk your bike down the hill to gentler terrain. Resource damage can result from riding on wet trails; call ahead to check on trail and road conditions. Wait until the spring thaw is complete and trails are dry before visiting mountainous regions. Pack out your own trash, and remove other people's litter when possible.

Become an informed participant and get involved in managing the lands you use for recreation.   Many groups are active in trail building and maintenance efforts. Non-ATB off-road-vehicle users and equestrians have a record of involvement that speaks well of their concern for public lands. As newcomers, mountain bikers need to make an extra effort to get involved in volunteer activities and in the managing of our common lands. Get in touch with a local cycling club or bike shop that works to keep trails open to mountain bikes and promotes responsible riding. Attend meetings where management and recreation plans are discussed. Ask to be placed on a mailing list for volunteer work to build or repair trails.

Southern California led the nation in embracing the use of mountain bikes, and thus understandably has been the first to experience the environmental damage and trail-user conflicts brought on by careless riding. We hope that our suggestions will help minimize these problems, and allow all of us—runners, hikers, equestrians, and bikers—to enjoy this fantastic countryside.

Laurie and Chris Leman

Introduction

TRAIL DESCRIPTION OUTLINE

Information on each trail in this book begins with a general description that includes length, configuration, scenery, highlights, trail conditions, and difficulty. Additional description is contained in eleven individual categories. The following will help you to understand all of the information provided.

Trail name: Trail names are as designated on USGS (United States Geological Survey) or Forest Service or other maps, and/or by local custom.

Length: The overall length of a trail is described in miles, unless stated otherwise.

Configuration: This is a description of the shape of each trail—whether the trail is a loop, out-and-back (that is, along the same route), figure-eight, trapezoid, isosceles triangle . . . , or if it connects with another trail described in the book.

Difficulty: This provides at a glance a description of the degree of physical exertion required to complete the ride, and the technical skill required to pedal it. Authors were asked to keep in mind the fact that all riders are not equal, and thus to gauge the trail in terms of how the middle-of-the-road rider—someone between the newcomer and Ned Overend—could handle the route. Comments about the trail's length, condition, and elevation change will also assist you in determining the difficulty of any trail relative to your own abilities.

Condition: Trails are described in terms of being paved, unpaved, sandy, hard-packed, washboarded, two- or four-wheel-drive, single-track, or double-track. All terms that might be unfamiliar to the first-time mountain biker are defined in the Glossary.

Scenery: Here you will find a general description of the natural surroundings during the seasons most riders pedal the trail, and a suggestion of what is to be found at special times (like great fall foliage or cacti in bloom).

Highlights: Towns, major water crossings, historical sites, etc., are listed.

General location: This category describes where the trail is located in reference to a nearby town or other landmark.

Elevation change: Unless stated otherwise, the figure provided is the total gain and loss of elevation along the trail. In regions where the elevation variation is not extreme, the route is described in a more general manner as flat, rolling, or as possessing short steep climbs or descents.

Season: This is the best time of year to pedal the route, taking into account trail condition (for example, when it will not be muddy), riding comfort (when the weather is too hot, cold, or wet), and local hunting seasons.

Note: Because the exact opening and closing dates of deer, elk, moose, and antelope seasons often change from year to year, it is suggested that riders check with the local Fish and Game department, or call a sporting goods store (or any place that sells hunting licenses) in a nearby town. Wear bright clothes in fall, and don't wear suede jackets while in the saddle. Hunter's-orange tape on the helmet is also a good idea.

Services: This category is of primary importance in guides for paved-road tourers, but is far less crucial to most mountain bike trail descriptions because there are usually no services whatsoever to be found. Authors have noted when water is available on desert or long mountain routes, and have listed the availability of food, lodging, campgrounds, and bike shops. If all these services are present, you will find only the words "All services available in . . ."

Hazards: Special hazards like steep cliffs, great amounts of deadfall, or barbed-wire fences very close to the trail are noted here.

Rescue index: Determining how far one is from help on any particular trail can be difficult due to the backcountry nature of most mountain bike rides. Authors therefore state the proximity of homes or Forest Service outposts, nearby roads where one might hitch a ride, or the likelihood of other bikers being encountered on the trail. Phone numbers of local sheriff departments or hospitals have not been provided because, again, phones are almost never available. Besides, if a phone is reached the local operator will connect you with emergency services.

Land status: This category provides information regarding whether the trail crosses land operated by the Forest Service, Bureau of Land Management, a city, state, or national park, whether it crosses private land whose owner (at the time the author did the research) allowed mountain bikers right of passage, and so on.

Note: Authors have been extremely careful to offer only those routes that are open to bikers and are legal to ride. However, because land ownership changes over time, and because the land-use controversy created by mountain bikes still has not subsided totally, it is the duty of each cyclist to look for and to heed signs warning against trail use. Don't expect this book to get you off the hook when you're facing some small-town judge for pedaling past a "Biking Prohibited" sign erected the day before. Look for these signs, read them, and heed the advice. And remember there's always another trail.

Maps: The maps in this book have been produced with great care, and in conjunction with the trail-following suggestions will help you stay on course. But as every experienced mountain biker knows, things can get tricky in the backcountry. It is therefore strongly suggested that you avail yourself of the detailed information found in the 7.5 minute series USGS (United States Geological Survey) topographic maps. In some cases, authors have found that specific Forest Service or other maps may be more useful than the USGS quads, and tell how to obtain them.

Finding the trail: Detailed information on how to reach the trailhead, and where to park your car, is provided here.

Sources of additional information: Here you will find the address and/or phone number of a bike shop, governmental agency, or other source from which trail information can be obtained.

Notes on the trail: This is where you are guided carefully through any portions of the trail that are particularly difficult to follow. The authors also may add information about the route that does not fit easily into the other categories.

ABBREVIATIONS

The following road-designation abbreviations are used in the *America by Mountain Bike* series:

CR	County Road
FR	Farm Route
FS	Forest Service road
I-	Interstate
IR	Indian Route
US	United States highway

State highways are designated with the appropriate two-letter state abbreviation, followed by the road number. *Example:* UT 6 = Utah State Highway 6.

Postal Service two-letter state code:

AL	Alabama	ME	Maine
AK	Alaska	MD	Maryland
AZ	Arizona	MA	Massachusetts
AR	Arkansas	MI	Michigan
CA	California	MN	Minnesota
CO	Colorado	MS	Mississippi
CT	Connecticut	MO	Missouri
DE	Delaware	MT	Montana
DC	District of Columbia	NE	Nebraska
FL	Florida	NV	Nevada
GA	Georgia	NH	New Hampshire
HI	Hawaii	NJ	New Jersey
ID	Idaho	NM	New Mexico
IL	Illinois	NY	New York
IN	Indiana	NC	North Carolina
IA	Iowa	ND	North Dakota
KS	Kansas	OH	Ohio
KY	Kentucky	OK	Oklahoma
LA	Louisiana	OR	Oregon

PA	Pennsylvania	VT	Vermont
RI	Rhode Island	VA	Virginia
SC	South Carolina	WA	Washington
SD	South Dakota	WV	West Virginia
TN	Tennessee	WI	Wisconsin
TX	Texas	WY	Wyoming
UT	Utah		

TOPOGRAPHIC MAPS

The maps in this book, when used in conjunction with the route directions present in each chapter, will in most instances be sufficient to get you to the trail and keep you on it. However, these maps cannot begin to provide the detailed information found in the 7.5 minute series USGS (United States Geological Survey) topographic maps. Recognizing how indispensable these are to bikers and hikers alike, many bike shops and sporting goods stores now carry topos of the local area.

But if you're brand new to mountain biking you might be wondering "What's a topographic map?" In short, these differ from standard "flat" maps because they indicate not only linear distance, but elevation as well. One glance at a topo will show you the difference, for "contour lines" are spread across the map like dozens of intricate spider webs. Each contour line represents a particular elevation, and each topo has written at its base a particular "contour interval" designation. Yes, it sounds confusing if you're new to the lingo, but it truly is a simple and wonderfully helpful system. Keep reading.

Let's assume that the 7.5 minute series topo before us says "Contour Interval 40 feet." And that the short trail we'll be pedaling is two inches in length on the map, and crosses five contour lines between its beginning and end. What do we know? Well, because the linear scale of this series is two thousand feet to the inch (roughly 2¾ inches representing a mile), we know our trail is approximately four-fifths of a mile long (2" × 2000'). But we also know we'll be climbing or descending 200 vertical feet (5 contour lines × 40 feet each) over that distance. And the elevation designations written on occasional contour lines will tell us if we're heading up or down.

The authors of this series warn their readers of upcoming terrain, but only a detailed topo gives you the information that enables you to pinpoint your position exactly on a map, steer you toward optional trails and roads nearby, plus let you know at a glance if you'll be pedaling hard to take them. It's a lot of information for a very low cost. In fact, the only drawback with topos is their size—several feet square. I've tried rolling them into tubes, folding them carefully, even cutting them into blocks and photocopying the pieces. Any of these systems is a

The Pacific Ocean from a ridge top in Moro Canyon.

pain, but no matter how you pack the maps you'll be happy they're along. And you'll be even happier if you pack a compass as well.

Major universities and some public libraries also carry topos; you might try photocopying the ones you need to avoid the cost of buying them. But if you want your own and can't find them locally, write to:

USGS Map Sales
Box 25286
Denver, CO 80225

Ask for an index while you're at it, plus a price list and a copy of the booklet *Topographic Maps*. In minutes you'll be reading them like a pro.

A second excellent series of maps available to mountain bikers is distributed by the United States Forest Service. If your trail runs through an area designated as a national forest, look in the phone book (white pages) under the United States Government listings, find the Department of Agriculture heading, and then run your finger through that section until you find the Forest Service. Give them a call and they'll provide the address of the regional Forest Service office, from which you can obtain the appropriate map.

LAND-USE CONTROVERSY

A few years ago I wrote a long piece on this issue for *Sierra Magazine* and called literally dozens of government land managers, game wardens, mountain bikers, and local officials to get a feeling for how ATBs were being welcomed on the trails. All that I've seen personally since, and heard from my authors, indicates there hasn't been much change. Which means we're still considered the new kid on the block, that we have less right to the trails than horses and hikers, and that we're excluded from many areas including:

a) wilderness areas
b) national parks (except on roads, and those paths specifically marked "bike path")
c) national monuments (except on roads open to the public)
d) most state parks and monuments (except on roads, and those paths specifically marked "bike path")
e) an increasing number of urban and county parks, especially in California (except on roads, and those areas specifically marked "bike path")

Frankly, I have little difficulty with these exclusions, and would in fact restrict our presence from some trails I've ridden (one time) due to the environmental damage and chance of blind-siding the many walkers and hikers I encountered along the way. But these are my personal views. They should not be interpreted as those of the authors and are mentioned here only as a way of introducing the land-use problem and the varying positions on it, which even mountain bikers hold.

You can do your part in keeping us from being excluded from even more trails by riding responsibly. Many local and national off-road bicycle organizations have been formed with exactly this in mind, and one of the largest—NORBA, the National Off-Road Bicycle Association—offers the following code of behavior for mountain bikers:

1. I will yield the right of way to other non-motorized recreationists. I realize that people judge all cyclists by my actions.
2. I will slow down and use caution when approaching or overtaking another person and will make my presence known well in advance.
3. I will maintain control of my speed at all times and will approach turns in anticipation of meeting someone around the bend.
4. I will stay on designated trails to avoid trampling native vegetation and minimize potential erosion to trails by not using muddy trails or short-cutting switchbacks.
5. I will not disturb wildlife or livestock.
6. I will not litter. I will pack out what I pack in, and pack out more than my share whenever possible.

Parked below 13,000-foot Wheeler Ridge.

7. I will respect public and private property, including trail use signs, no trespassing signs, and I will leave gates as I have found them.
8. I will always be self-sufficient and my destination and travel speed will be determined by my ability, my equipment, the terrain, the present and potential weather conditions.
9. I will not travel solo when bikepacking in remote areas. I will leave word of my destination and when I plan to return.

10. I will observe the practice of minimum impact bicycling by "taking only pictures and memories and leaving only waffle prints."
11. I will always wear a helmet whenever I ride.

Now, I have a problem with some of these—number nine, for instance. The most enjoyable mountain biking I've ever done has been solo. And as for leaving word of destination and time of return, I've enjoyed living in such a way that I can say, "I'm off to pedal Colorado. See you in the fall." Of course it's senseless to take needless risks, and I plan a ride and pack my gear with this in mind. But for me number nine smacks too much of the "never-out-of-touch" mentality. And getting away from civilization, deep into the wilds, is for many people what mountain biking's all about.

All in all, however, theirs is a good list, and surely we mountain bikers would be liked more, and excluded less, if we followed the suggestions. But let me offer a "code of ethics" I much prefer, one given to cyclists by Utah's Wasatch-Cache National Forest office.

Study a Forest Map Before You Ride
Currently, bicycles are permitted on roads and developed trails within the Wasatch-Cache National Forest except in designated wilderness. If your route crosses private land, it is your responsibility to obtain right-of-way permission from the land owner.

Keep Groups Small
Riding in large groups degrades the outdoor experience for others, can disturb wildlife, and usually leads to greater resource damage.

Avoid Riding on Wet Trails
Bicycle tires leave ruts in wet trails. These ruts concentrate runoff and accelerate erosion. Postponing a ride when the trails are wet will preserve the trails for future use.

Stay on Roads and Trails
Riding cross-country destroys vegetation and damages the soil.

Always Yield to Others
Trails are shared by hikers, horses and bicycles. Move off the trail to allow horses to pass and stop to allow hikers adequate room to share the trail. Simply yelling "Bicycle!" is not acceptable.

Control Your Speed
Excessive speed endangers yourself and other forest users.

Avoid Wheel Lock-up and Spin-out
Steep terrain is especially vulnerable to trail wear. Locking brakes on steep descents or when stopping needlessly damages trails. If a slope is steep enough to require locking wheels and skidding, dismount and walk your

bicycle. Likewise, if an ascent is so steep your rear wheel slips and spins, dismount and walk your bicycle.

Protect Waterbars and Switchbacks

Waterbars, the rock and log drains built to direct water off trails, protect trails from erosion. When you encounter a waterbar, ride directly over the top or dismount and walk your bicycle. Riding around the ends of waterbars destroys them and speeds erosion. Skidding around switchback corners shortens trail life. Slow down for switchback corners and keep your wheels rolling.

If You Abuse It, You Lose It

Mountain bikers are relative newcomers to the forest and must prove themselves responsible trail users. By following the guidelines above, and by participating in trail maintenance service projects, bicyclists can help avoid closures which would prevent them from using trails.

I've never seen a better trail-etiquette list for mountain bikers. So have fun. Be careful. And don't screw things up for the next rider.

HITTING THE TRAIL

Once again, because this is a "where-to," not a "how-to" guide, the following will be brief. If you're a veteran trail rider these suggestions might serve to remind you of something you've forgotten to pack. If you're a newcomer, they might convince you to think twice before hitting the backcountry unprepared.

Water: I've heard the questions dozens of times. "How much is enough? One bottle? Two? Three?! But think of all that extra weight!" Well, one simple physiological fact should convince you to err on the side of excess when it comes to determining how much water to pack: a human working hard in ninety-degree temperature needs approximately ten quarts of fluids every day. Ten quarts. That's two and a half gallons—*twelve* large water bottles, or *sixteen* small ones. And with water weighing in at approximately eight pounds per gallon, a one-day supply comes to a whopping twenty pounds.

In other words, pack along two or three bottles even for short rides. And make sure you can purify the water found along the trail on longer routes. When writing of those routes where this could be of critical importance, the authors have provided information on where water can be found near the trail—if it can be found at all. But drink it untreated and you run the risk of disease. [See *Giardia* in the Glossary.]

One sure way to kill both the bacteria and viruses in water is to boil it for ten minutes, plus one minute more for each one thousand feet of elevation above sea level. Right. That's just how you want to spend your time on a bike ride. Besides, who wants to carry a stove, or denude the countryside stoking bonfires to boil water?

Luckily, there is a better way. Many riders pack along the effective, inexpensive, and only slightly distasteful tetraglycine hydroperiodide tablets (sold under the names of Potable Aqua, Globaline, Coughlan's, and others). Some invest in portable, lightweight purifiers that filter out the crud. Yes, purifying water with tablets or filters is a bother. But catch a case of Giardia sometime and you'll understand why it's worth the trouble.

Tools: Ever since my first cross-country tour in '65 I've been kidded about the number of tools I pack on the trail. And so I will exit entirely from this discussion by providing a list compiled by two mechanic (and mountain biker) friends of mine. After all, since they make their livings fixing bikes, and get their kicks by riding them, who could be a better source?

The following is suggested as an absolute minimum:

> tire levers
> spare tube and patch kit
> air pump
> allen wrenches (3, 4, 5, and 6 mm)
> six-inch crescent (adjustable-end) wrench
> small flat-blade screwdriver
> chain rivet tool
> spoke wrench

But their personal tool pouches carried on the trail contain, in addition to the above:

> channel locks (small)
> air gauge
> tire valve cap (the metal kind, with a valve-stem remover)
> baling wire (ten or so inches, for temporary repairs)
> duct tape (small roll for temporary repairs or tire boot)
> boot material (small piece of old tire or a large tube patch)
> · spare chain link
> rear derailleur pulley
> spare nuts and bolts
> paper towel and tube of waterless hand cleaner

First-aid kit: My personal kit contains the following, sealed inside double zip-lock bags:

> sunscreen
> aspirin

butterfly closure bandages
band-aids
gauze compress pads (a half-dozen 4″×4″)
gauze (one roll)
ace bandages or Spenco joint wraps
Benadryl (an antihistamine to guard against possible allergic reactions)
water purification tablets
moleskin/Spenco "Second Skin"
hydrogen peroxide/iodine/Mercurochrome (some kind of antiseptic)
snakebite kit

Final considerations: The authors of this series have done a good job in suggesting that specific items be packed for certain trails—like raingear in particular seasons, a hat and gloves for mountain passes, or shades for desert jaunts. Heed their warnings, and think ahead. Good luck.

Dennis Coello
Salt Lake City

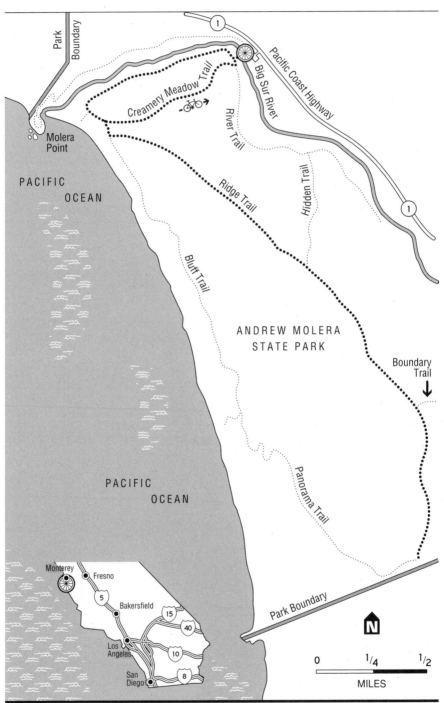

RIDE 1   *RIDGE TRAIL / ANDREW MOLERA STATE PARK*

This is a strenuous out-and-back ride with a short loop around Creamery Meadow. It is 7.8 miles long and is fairly technical (due to a loose, rocky surface). All but the strongest riders with the lightest bicycles will do some walking up the ridge line. The downhill return is also difficult. It is steep and bumpy—a very rough ride. The riding around Creamery Meadow is easy. Ridge Trail is a four-wheel-drive dirt road that varies from fair to good condition. There are loose rocks on the steeper sections.

Cyclists tackling this tough little ride will reap huge rewards. Here, foggy days can be looked upon as wonderful opportunities. You may be able to climb above the coastal layer to sunshine and surreal scenery. On clear days the view down the coast to Big Sur is phenomenal.

General location: Begins at the parking area of Andrew Molera State Park, 22 miles south of Carmel on the Pacific Coast Highway (CA 1).
Elevation change: The ride begins 100' above sea level and follows mostly level terrain to mile 1.1 where you begin climbing on Ridge Trail. Ridge Trail ends at 1,100' at mile 3.9. Rolling terrain adds some 200' of additional climbing to the ride. Total elevation gain: 1,200'.
Season: Year-round. But the best riding is spring through fall. Due to the park's proximity to the ocean, daytime temperatures can be low and fog is common. Carry extra clothing for sudden changes in the weather. Winter and spring can be rainy.
Services: Water was not available at Andrew Molera State Park at the time of our research, but a drinking water system was being installed. All services are available in the community of Big Sur, approximately 3 miles south on CA 1.
Hazards: There is a footbridge over the Big Sur River near the trailhead. The bridge is built out of 2 wooden planks, so walk or carry your bike across. Control your speed while descending on Ridge Trail. It is rough and rocky in places. Watch for other trail users.
Rescue index: Help is available in the community of Big Sur.
Land status: State park.
Maps: A good map of the park may be obtained at the entrance station.
Finding the trail: From points north, drive 22 miles south of Carmel on CA 1 to Andrew Molera State Park on the right (west) side of the highway. From points south, drive 3 miles north of the community of Big Sur on CA 1 to Andrew Molera State Park on the left (west) side of the highway. Enter and park in the parking lot near the picnic area and trailhead.

Fog rolling in north of Big Sur.

Sources of additional information:

Andrew Molera State Park
c/o Pfeiffer Big Sur State Park
Big Sur, CA 93920

Notes on the trail: Begin at the hiking trailhead (not the trailhead for the camp-ground) and cross the wooden bridge. Ride to the main trail at a "T" intersection and turn right. Stay right at the next "Y" intersection. Just before you've ped-aled 1 mile you'll see a sign for Beach Trail; turn left to continue on Creamery Meadow Trail. Soon after, turn right uphill at the sign for Ridge Trail. Continue straight on Ridge Trail as Bluff Trail goes right toward the ocean (no bikes). Con-tinue on Ridge Trail past Hidden Trail to the left (no bikes). Continue straight as North Boundary Trail goes left (no bikes). You will reach the top of the climb and a fence at 3.9 miles—turn around and return the way you came. When you come again to the Creamery Meadow Trail, follow it to the right around the meadow. Turn left at the "Y" intersection before the barbed wire fence to continue around the meadow. In .1 mile turn hard right and follow the trail back across the bridge to the parking area and your vehicle.

Another place within the park you may wish to explore is Molera Point. Reach this portion of the park's headlands by following Beach Trail from the park-ing lot. The view from the point is excellent, especially at sunset. This is a fine location for whale watching, which is generally at its best in January.

RIDE 2 *CENTRAL COAST RIDGE ROAD*

This is an out-and-back, 10.8-mile round-trip ride. It requires little technical skill, the terrain is generally easy-to-moderate, and there is plenty of shade. The unpaved, two-wheel-drive road is in good condition. After approximately four miles you encounter a one-quarter-mile steep hill that contains some loose rock and rutting.

Central Coast Ridge Road winds back and forth along the ridge, providing alternate views of the Pacific Ocean to the west and the interior valleys and mountains of the Ventana Wilderness to the east. A four-mile out-and-back hike from the turnaround point to Cone Peak is well worth the extra time and effort. The hiking trail is basically a long uphill meander, with the steepest section being the last one-quarter mile. The view of the coastline from the lookout tower is excellent. To the south is Point Sal; to the north is Big Sur.

General location: Begins off of Nacimiento-Fergusson Road, 7.5 miles east of California State Highway 1 (approximately 40 miles north of San Simeon).

Elevation change: The ride begins at 2,660' of elevation, passes San Antonio hiking trail at the 4-mile point at 3,200', and ends at a high point of 4,150' at the trail to Cone Peak. The hike tops out at 5,155'. Total elevation gain: 1,490' (hike not included).

Season: Year-round. Wildflower displays in the spring can be outstanding. Dry conditions can create extreme fire danger and road closures. Winter months can be wet and roads may be closed to minimize erosion. Check with the Forest Service concerning road conditions before embarking for the trailhead.

Services: There is no water on the ride. There is water available at the intersection of CA 1 and Nacimiento-Fergusson Road at Kirk Creek Campground. There are grocery stores in Gorda and Lucia. All services are available in San Simeon.

Hazards: Speed should be controlled on descents. Motor vehicles use this road, so be alert, especially on blind corners. Poison oak grows next to the trail to Cone Peak.

Rescue index: Help can be found in the town of Lucia.

Land status: National forest.

Maps: USGS 7.5 minute quadrangle map: Cone Peak.

Finding the trail: From points north, drive 4 miles south of Lucia on CA 1 and turn east on Nacimiento-Fergusson Road. From points south, drive 5 miles north of Gorda on CA 1 and turn east on Nacimiento-Fergusson Road. Follow Nacimiento-Fergusson Road for 7.5 miles to the ridge top and Central Coast Ridge Road. The ride begins at the sign indicating Central Coast Ridge Road #20S05. Park your vehicle in the pullout; do not block access to the road.

RIDE 2 *CENTRAL COAST RIDGE ROAD*

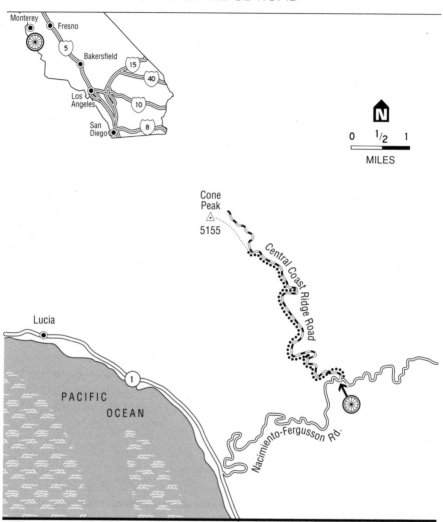

Sources of additional information:

Los Padres National Forest
Santa Lucia Ranger District
1616 Carlotti Drive
Santa Maria, CA 93454
(805) 925-9538

Chris cruising on the Central Coast Ridge Road.

Notes on the trail: Begin on Central Coast Ridge Road (Forest Service Road 20S05) in a northerly direction; a sign reads "Vincente Flats Trail 4, San Antonio Trail 4, Cone Peak Trail 6." Follow the main road to Cone Peak Trail on the left. Return the way you came.

The Central Coast Ridge Road runs through the Ventana Wilderness Area. No bicycles are permitted on trails leading off the main road. If you travel on Cone Peak Trail, leave your bike at the trailhead.

RIDE 3   *BLUFF TRAIL / MONTANA DE ORO STATE PARK*

This is an easy 3.3-mile loop. The ride follows a hard-packed dirt trail in good condition and pavement on Pecho Valley Road.

Bluff Trail is a fine spot for beginning mountain bikers to give off-road riding a try. It is also a wonderful warm-up for cyclists intent on riding the more advanced trails in the park. The trail skirts the coast and provides views of tidal pools, cliffs, and arches. Profuse wildflower displays and whale watching are seasonal bonuses.

RIDE 3 *BLUFF TRAIL / MONTANA DE ORO STATE PARK*

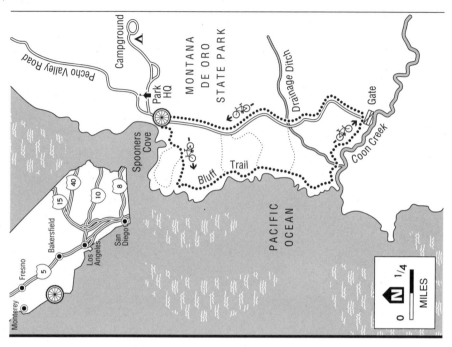

General location: Montana de Oro State Park is located approximately 20 miles west of San Luis Obispo on Pecho Valley Road.

Elevation change: Bluff Trail begins at 60′ of elevation and climbs very gently to 100′ at the trail's end. The paved portion of the loop involves several short climbs and reaches a high point of 200′. Total elevation gain: 140′.

Season: Year-round. Spring and early summer are especially beautiful, for wild-flowers and many kinds of birds are abundant. The wave-swept headlands of the park are a popular whale-watching spot in the winter.

Services: Water may be obtained at the park headquarters. The headquarters and a 50-site campground are located on the east side of Pecho Valley Road, 2.7 miles beyond the entrance sign for the park. All services are available in the community of San Luis Obispo.

Hazards: This trail is heavily used by hikers. Be especially alert when approaching children, for they can be unpredictable. Although the trail is adequately set back from the sheer cliffs of the coast, exercise caution when stopping for a closer look. Heed signs directing trail users to stay back from unstable edges. At mile 1.8 the trail crosses a drainage ditch with very steep sides. Beginners should walk their bikes at this point.

Rescue index: Help is available at the park headquarters.

Crashing surf from the bluffs of Montana de Oro State Park.

Land status: State park.

Maps: A good topographic map of the park may be purchased at the park headquarters.

Finding the trail: From points north, travel 3 miles south of San Luis Obispo on US 101 to the Los Osos/Baywood Park exit. From points south, travel 10 miles north of Grover City on US 101 to the Los Osos/Baywood Park exit. Exit and travel 12 miles northwest on Los Osos Valley Road. Los Osos Valley Road becomes Pecho Valley Road and enters the state park. Park headquarters is 2.7 miles past the Montana de Oro State Park entrance sign. The trailhead is signed on the west side of Pecho Valley Road, 100 yards south of the headquarters. There is a parking lot at the trailhead.

Sources of additional information:

> Montana de Oro State Park
> Los Osos, CA 93402
> (805) 528-0513

Notes on the trail: The ride starts at the trailhead signed as Bluff Trail. After a little more than .5 miles, you will come to a wooden bridge. Cross the bridge and stay right. Follow Bluff Trail south as it parallels the coast. After 2 miles of riding you reach a parking lot, picnic tables, and pit toilets. Turn left to return on the paved road to your vehicle. Should you decide to forego completion of the ride, several trails lead east from Bluff Trail and take you to Pecho Valley Road.

RIDE 4   *ISLAY CREEK TRAIL / MONTANA DE ORO STATE PARK*

This 8-mile loop is a relatively short but demanding ride. The first 3 miles on Islay Creek Road climb gently and steadily over several short, easy hills. Beginners should turn around here for a pleasant out-and-back trip, for after this the narrow, single-track East Boundary Trail climbs very steeply. It is rocky and sandy in places, and at times more closely resembles a ditch than a trail. On the single-track Ridge Trail you will encounter many ups and downs of varying technical and physical difficulty. Ridge Trail includes a variety of trail conditions. Expect rocky and sandy portions as well as some fine riding surfaces. There is some deep sand on the descent to paved Pecho Valley Road.

The views on this ride are outstanding. Nearing the top of East Boundary Trail you have a good view of Los Oso Valley and the community of Morro Bay. The rock at the bay's entrance is Morro Rock—one of nine volcanic plugs that lie in a line from Morro Bay to San Luis Obispo. You can see many of them from this vantage point. The coastal views from Hazard Peak are tremendous. In spring and early summer the wildflowers are particularly dazzling. Entire hillsides covered in monkey flowers and other yellow blooming plants inspired the name of this area—Montana de Oro, or Mountain of Gold.

General location: Approximately 17 miles west of San Luis Obispo.
Elevation change: The ride begins at 100' of elevation on Islay Creek Road. Following along the north side of Islay Creek you climb to 400' to meet East

RIDE 4 *ISLAY CREEK TRAIL / MONTANA DE ORO STATE PARK*

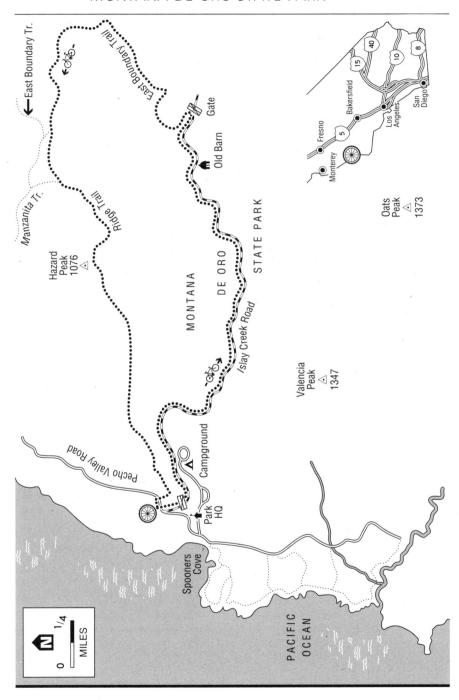

Boundary Trail. Short hills on Islay Creek Road add an estimated 75' of climbing. East Boundary Trail climbs to 1,000' and then descends to 900' before climbing again to 1,000'. East Boundary Trail intersects with Ridge Trail at 800'. Ups and downs along East Boundary Trail add an estimated 150' of climbing. On Ridge Trail you climb to the ride's high point at Hazard Peak—elevation 1,076'. Along the way to the peak you will ride many ascents and descents which add an estimated 400' to this climb. Descend from Hazard Peak to your vehicle at 100'. Total elevation gain: 1,901'.

Season: Year-round. The climate is mild in winter and cool in summer with considerable coastal fog and clouds. Whale watching is good from late November through January.

Services: All services are available in the community of Morro Bay. Water may be obtained at the park headquarters, located off Pecho Valley Road 2.7 miles beyond the park entrance sign.

Hazards: You will cross 2 cattle guards on Islay Creek Road. There is poison oak growing next to the trail in places, so watch out! Along East Boundary Trail you must be especially careful to avoid poison oak, for the trail is very narrow. Care must be taken ascending and descending rocky and sandy sections. Just past Hazard Peak you will approach remnants of a barbed wire fence. Just beyond the fence you must negotiate a particularly dangerous section of trail that passes over a rock outcropping. Stop, dismount, and survey the situation. Find a trail to the right that is more gradual than the main trail and provides better footing. Walk your bike around and rejoin the main trail. After this you will find some good trail but be ready for deep sandy spots. Nearing the bottom of Ridge Trail you will find water bars across the trail. Control your speed and watch for other trail users. This park is very popular with equestrians.

Rescue index: Help is available at the park headquarters, .2 miles south of the trailhead on Pecho Valley Road. Although this is a popular park, this particular route is not as heavily used as other trails in Montana de Oro State Park. You may not see anyone else on the trail. Park personnel patrol the trails, but not necessarily on a daily basis. Be prepared—carry adequate water, spare parts, and a first-aid kit. Beginners should travel with others.

Land status: State park.

Maps: A good topographic map of the park may be purchased at the park headquarters.

Finding the trail: From San Luis Obispo, travel south on CA 101 approximately 2 miles and take the Los Oso/Baywood Park exit. Travel northwest for 12 miles on Los Oso Valley Road (Los Oso Valley Road becomes Pecho Valley Road and enters Montana de Oro State Park). Follow Pecho Valley Road 2.5 miles beyond the entrance sign for the park to a parking area on the right (west) side of the road. Park here. Islay Creek Road begins across the road at a gate. Additional parking is available at the park headquarters, .2 miles further south on Pecho Valley Road.

Sources of additional information:

> Montana de Oro State Park
> Los Osos, CA 93402
> (805) 528-0513

Notes on the trail: Begin the ride at the gate at Islay Creek Road. Turn left after 3 miles onto East Boundary Trail. After 5 miles you'll come to a "Y" intersection and Ridge Trail. Turn left and follow Ridge Trail. Turn left after a quarter mile to stay on Ridge Trail at an intersection with Manzanita Trail. Follow Ridge Trail to reach Pecho Valley Road. Turn left to return to your vehicle.

You will encounter some tall water bars set across the route near the end of Ridge Trail. Do not go around them and cut a new trail. This defeats their purpose, which is to curtail erosion and preserve the existing trail. Hop them if you are experienced with this bike handling technique, or stop, dismount, and lift your bicycle over them.

RIDE 5   *BATES CANYON ROAD / SIERRA MADRE ROAD*

This is an out-and-back, 15-mile round-trip ride. Most of the pedaling is only moderately difficult, but there are several very steep sections. Overall, Bates Canyon Road is a long, difficult climb requiring good bike handling skills. Sierra Madre Road is less demanding—the climbing is mostly moderate. Both Bates Canyon and Sierra Madre Roads are unpaved, four-wheel-drive roads in fair condition. At the time of our research, the roads had been graded recently and were rock strewn and soft. We expect the road conditions to improve with time and traffic.

Bates Canyon Road, while a challenge to climb, provides access to one of the finest mountain bike routes around—Sierra Madre Road. For those seeking remoteness and uncrowded roads, this is a wonderful region to explore. From the top of the ridge you look down on the San Rafael Wilderness and across to the San Rafael Mountains. Those arriving via Santa Maria enjoy an added bonus— a lovely drive along a scenic stretch of CA 166.

General location: The ride begins at Bates Canyon Campground at the end of Cottonwood Canyon Road (approximately 50 miles east of Santa Maria) in the Los Padres National Forest.

Elevation change: Bates Canyon Road starts at 2,900′ and climbs to 5,200′ to meet Sierra Madre Road. Sierra Madre Road follows the ridge to the turnaround point of the ride, Hot Peak, at 5,587′. Total elevation gain: 2,687′.

Season: Spring through fall. High temperatures in the summer can make this

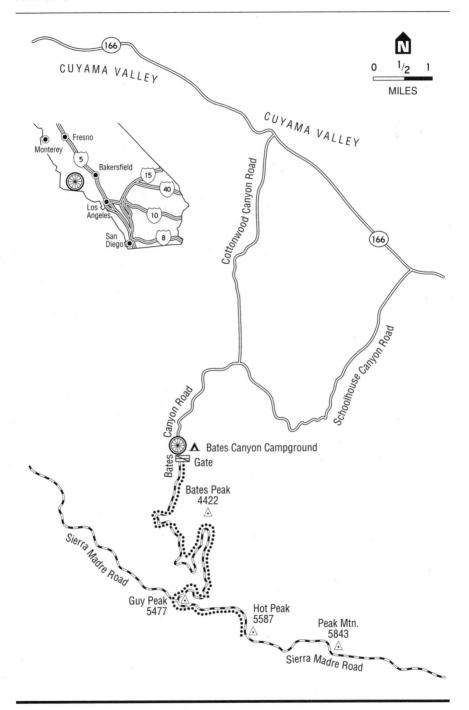

Looking down Bates Canyon.

an uncomfortable ride and insects can be bothersome. Rain or snow may make these roads impassable in the winter.

Services: No water is available on the ride. Piped water is available at the start of the ride at Bates Canyon Campground. Limited services are present in the small town of New Cuyama, 12 miles east of Cottonwood Canyon Road on CA 166. All services are available in Santa Maria.

Hazards: The road surface may be rough and can cause handling problems. Although this is a relatively remote area, you still must expect others to be around the next bend in the road. Motor vehicles are permitted; take care on blind corners. Be prepared for sudden weather changes; a ridge can be a dangerous place in a thunderstorm. Poison oak is abundant in Bates Canyon.

Rescue index: Help is available in New Cuyama or Santa Maria. Ride with others who may be able to provide a first response in an emergency.

Land status: National forest.

Maps: USGS 7.5 minute quadrangle maps: Bates Canyon and Peak Mountain.

Finding the trail: From US 101 in Santa Maria, travel east on CA 166 for 40 miles to Cottonwood Canyon Road on the right (south) side of the highway. From New Cuyama, travel 12 miles west on CA 166 to Cottonwood Canyon on the left (south) side of the highway. Signs on both sides of the highway direct you towards White Oak Station (no longer in use) and Bates Canyon Campground. Follow Cottonwood Canyon Road 6.5 miles to White Oak Station, where you can park your car. Bates Canyon Campground and the start of the ride is a quarter mile further down the paved road.

Sources of additional information:

Los Padres National Forest Supervisor's Office
6144 Calle Real
Goleta, CA 93117
(805) 683-6711

Santa Lucia Ranger District
1616 Carlotti Drive
Santa Maria, CA 93454
(805) 925-9538

Notes on the trail: From Bates Canyon Campground, follow the unsigned, paved Bates Canyon Road (Forest Service Road 11N01) as it passes behind the pit toilets. Follow it to the end of the pavement. You will immediately pass a sign indicating that you are on Bates Canyon Road, and will soon ride through an open gate. After approximately 4 miles the road makes a sweeping right turn as you pass Bates Peak. Turn left after 2 more miles onto unmarked Sierra Madre Road (which runs along the top of the ridge). You will reach Hot Peak in 1.5 miles. Turn around and return the way you came.

RIDE 6 *WILDHORSE / ZACA PEAK*

Here is a good trip for strong cyclists, or moderately strong cyclists with an excess amount of energy. It is an out-and-back ride and covers 18.5 miles round-trip. There are some long, steep hills and some sections that may bring the words "roller coaster" to mind. Good bike handling skills are needed to negotiate rough ascents and descents. Catway and Zaca Ridge roads are unpaved (hard-packed dirt and rock base) four-wheel-drive roads. They are in good condition, though the steeper hills have some loose rocks and gravel. The road out to Zaca Peak is in fair condition with loose rocks and ruts.

Exceptional views of the Santa Ynez Valley and the San Rafael Wilderness Area, combined with good roads, challenging terrain, and an abundance of wild-flowers, make this an excellent ride. The drive on Figueroa Mountain Road to the start of the ride is also lovely. The road winds past peaceful ranch lands and gnarled old oak trees before snaking steeply up Figueroa Mountain.

General location: The ride starts on Figueroa Mountain, approximately 10 miles northeast of the Santa Ynez Valley (50 miles southeast of Santa Maria).
Elevation change: Catway Road begins at approximately 3,670' and climbs to 4,390' in 2.3 miles. Catway then nosedives to 4,100'. This is followed by a lot of up-and-down riding. About 5 miles in, a high point of 4,400' is obtained.

RIDE 6 *WILDHORSE / ZACA PEAK*

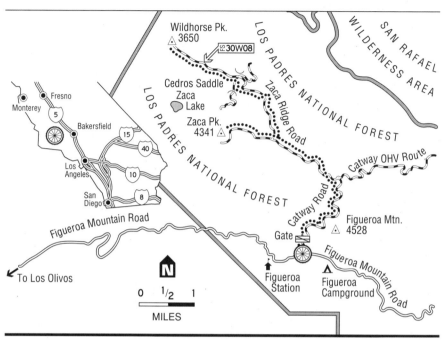

Then the road descends to 3,600' at Cedros Saddle. From the saddle, the route follows a ridge and rolling terrain to 3,650' at Wildhorse Peak. On the return, Cedros Saddle is passed and the road ascends back to 4,400'. A side trip to Zaca Peak begins at approximately 4,200'. This road drops to 4,000' and then climbs back to 4,200'. The trip ends with rolling topography to 4,390', and then a nice descent to your vehicle. Shorter hills add about 500' to this excursion. Total elevation gain: 3,060'.

Season: Early spring through fall. The altitude of this ride makes for pleasant riding in the summer.

Services: There is no water on this ride. Water is available on a seasonal basis at Figueroa Campground (.5 miles east of Catway Road on Figueroa Mountain Road). All services can be obtained in Los Olivos.

Hazards: There are loose rocks and gravel on the steeper hills. Motor vehicles are permitted on the roads described in this ride. Expect sudden weather changes and carry extra clothing.

Rescue index: Help can be found in Los Olivos. Help may be available at Figueroa Station (1 mile west of the start of the ride on Figueroa Mountain Road).

Land status: National forest.

Shady climbing on Catway Road.

Maps: USGS 7.5 minute quadrangle maps: Zaca Lake, Bald Mountain, Figueroa Mountain, and Los Olivos.

Finding the trail: From Los Olivos, drive north on Figueroa Mountain Road. Follow Figueroa Mountain Road for 13 miles to Figueroa Station. Continue 1 mile beyond Figueroa Station on Figueroa Mountain Road to Catway Road on the left (north) side of the road. Catway Road is marked by a sign that reads

"Gate Temporarily Closed When Road Is Wet." Park here, but do not block the gate or access to the road.

Sources of additional information:

Los Padres National Forest
6144 Calle Real
Goleta, CA 93117
(805) 683-6711

Notes on the trail: Follow Catway Road about 2.5 miles to an intersection. Turn left to stay on the main road (now Zaca Ridge Road), as Catway OHV Route goes right toward Davey Brown Campground. After another 2 miles, continue straight as a road goes left to Zaca Peak and Zaca Lake (this ride description will have you follow this road to the south side of Zaca Peak on the return). Ride 1.5 miles farther to Cedros Saddle (an intersection of trails). At the saddle, continue straight on the main road. Pedal 2 more miles to the end of the road at unmarked Wildhorse Peak (reached after 8 miles of riding). Return the way you came, passing Cedros Saddle, and turn right at the sign for Zaca Peak. After about 1.5 miles, the road ends at a spot that offers nice views to the south. Return the way you came.

RIDE 7 *LITTLE PINE MOUNTAIN*

This is an excellent ride for the strong cyclist who wants a good workout as well as great views. It is an out-and-back ride (23.4 miles round-trip), and is strenuous. The first 1.5 miles provide a good warm-up with easy to moderate climbing and some shade. From this point you'll face ten miles of moderately steep to steep climbing to the road's crest. This long exposed climb is broken up by some easier stretches and some short descents. All of the cycling is on unpaved four-wheel-drive roads in generally good condition. Good bike handling technique is necessary for climbing and descending over intermittent loose and soft surfaces.

Rounding a bend after 5.5 miles you will see the chalk bluffs on Little Pine Mountain and the long, exposed switchbacks that you'll be climbing soon. Riding up the switchbacks provides an outstanding view. Leave your bike at Happy Hollow Camp and follow the hiking trail to the west one-quarter mile for another great vista. The return descent is a thrill.

General location: Begins in the Lower Santa Ynez Recreation Area in the Los Padres National Forest, approximately 15 miles north of Santa Barbara.
Elevation change: The ride begins at 1,200′ in Upper Oso Campground and climbs to a high point of 4,400′ near the top of Little Pine Mountain. Undulating

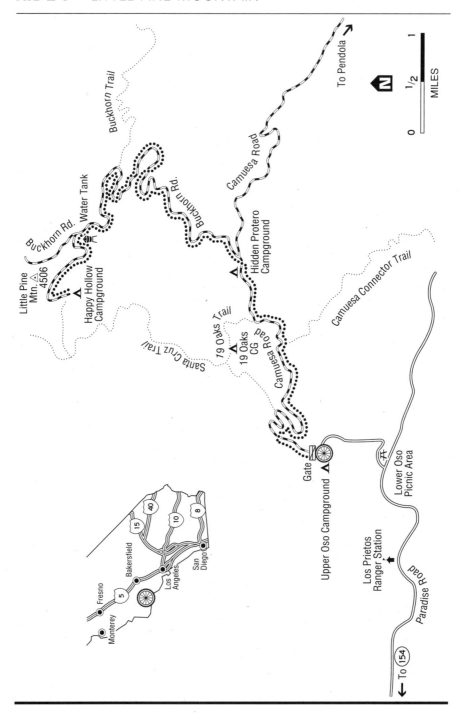

The long and winding road down Little Pine Mountain.

terrain adds an estimated 100′ of additional climbing to the ride. Total elevation gain: 3,300′.

Season: Early spring and late fall are the best riding seasons for the Lower Santa Ynez Recreation Area. It is possible to ride throughout the year, though high temperatures in summer and inclement weather in winter are limiting factors.

Services: There is no water available on the ride. Water may be obtained at Upper Oso Campground; take plenty. A general store is located on Paradise Road near CA 154. All services are available in Santa Barbara.

Hazards: The road is shared with off-road vehicles and care must be taken on blind corners. Between 1 and 3 miles along the route the road is particularly narrow and winding. Control your speed on the descent.

Rescue index: Help is available at the Los Prietos Ranger Station on Paradise Road (approximately 2.8 miles southwest of the start of the ride).

Land status: National forest.

Maps: The "Mountain Bicycle Guide" available at the Los Prietos Ranger Station is an excellent guide to this trail.

Finding the trail: Follow CA 154 north from Santa Barbara for approximately 10 miles; turn right onto Paradise Road. Follow for 5 miles to Lower Oso Picnic Area and turn left, then continue 1.3 miles to Upper Oso Campground. Parking is permitted near the locked gate for the trailhead. Overnight parking is permitted.

Sources of additional information:

Los Prietos Ranger Station
Star Route
Santa Barbara, CA 93105
(805) 967-3481

Notes on the trail: Begin this ride on the unsigned Camuesa Road at the locked gate at the north end of Upper Oso Campground. After .7 miles a side trail is signed Santa Cruz Trail; cycling is permitted on this hiking trail to Little Pine Mountain, but we do not recommend it as it is narrow, rocky, and steep. Continue on Camuesa Road as Camuesa Road Connector Trail goes to the right after two more miles. Continue past 19 Oaks Trail on the left, and at the intersection 2 miles farther, turn left onto Buckhorn Road toward Little Pine Mountain; Camuesa Road goes right to Pendola. Nine miles into the ride, where the Buckhorn Hiking Trail turns right, you will continue on the main road. Just past a water tank a mile farther on, turn left to Happy Hollow Camp as Buckhorn Road continues straight. In another 1.5 miles you will reach Happy Hollow Camp where you will find picnic tables, shade, and ants. Return the way you came.

RIDE 8 *ROMERO CANYON*

This out-and-back, 13.8-mile round-trip is an uphill workout. The climb to the turnaround point is long and moderately difficult. The road is steep for the first half mile and then moderate after the second creek crossing. The return is fast and technically demanding. Romero Road is unmaintained and has been closed to motor vehicles since the 1970s. At times it seems like a road and at other times it narrows to a single-track trail. The single-track sections are generally rough with loose and embedded rocks. The dirt road sections are in fair condition with some loose rocks.

The route climbs through Romero Canyon and deposits you on the Coast Ridge at Romero Saddle. Excellent ocean views are a bonus as you grind it out to reach the top. Romero Road is the most direct path out of Santa Barbara and into the backcountry. Longer day trips and overnighters can be made from Romero Saddle.

General location: Romero Road (Forest Service Road 5N15) starts from Bella Vista Road in Montecito, approximately 10 miles east of Santa Barbara.
Elevation change: The trip begins at 1,300′ and climbs to a high point of 3,100′ at Romero Saddle. Total elevation gain: 1800′.
Season: Year-round. This ride can be a sweaty one, even in winter. Carry a dry shirt and a windbreaker.

RIDE 8 *ROMERO CANYON*

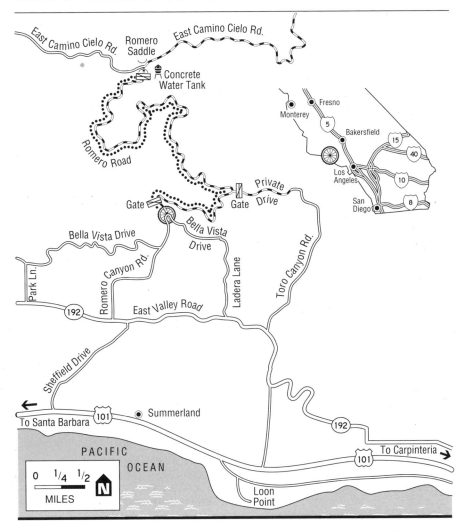

Services: There is no water on this ride. All services are available in Santa Barbara and surrounding communities.

Hazards: Romero Road is a very popular hiking and cycling route. Watch for other trail users. Control your speed while descending and approach corners with care.

Rescue index: Help can be found in Santa Barbara.

Land status: National forest.

The Pacific Ocean and the Channel Islands from a Romero Canyon viewpoint.

Maps: Map #4 of the Santa Barbara County Recreational Map Series—"Santa Barbara Mountain Biking Routes"—is an excellent guide to this and other trails in the area. This map can be purchased at district offices of the Los Padres National Forest or by writing the publisher: McNally and Loftin, 5390 Overpass Road, Santa Barbara, CA 93111.

Finding the trail: From Santa Barbara, follow US 101 south to the exit for Sheffield Drive. Follow Sheffield Drive north for 1.5 miles to East Valley Road. Turn left onto East Valley Road, and then immediately turn right onto Romero Canyon Road. Follow Romero Canyon Road north for 1.5 miles and turn right onto Bella Vista Drive. Take Bella Vista Drive .3 miles to a red steel gate on the left side of the road. The red gate marks the start of Romero Road. Park your car here. Do not block access to Romero Road.

Sources of additional information:

Los Padres National Forest
Santa Barbara Ranger District
Los Prietos, Star Route
Santa Barbara, CA 93105
(805) 967-3481

Notes on the trail: Begin the ride at the red gate at Romero Road and Bella Vista Drive. After 2 miles stay left, as the road to the right (blocked by a blue gate) leads to a private residence. In approximately 2 more miles you come to some signs that indicate you are on your way to Romero Saddle and Camino Cielo Road. There is also a sign that directs hikers on Romero Trail to Ocean-view Trail and Blue Canyon Trail. Continue straight on the main road toward Romero Saddle. Two miles beyond the signs you reach an open area where there is a shot-up water tank on the hillside to your right. Continue straight. Soon you arrive at a locked gate that can be ridden around on the left. Just past the gate is Romero Saddle and East Camino Cielo Road at a concrete water tank (6.9 miles into the ride). Return the way you came.

RIDE 9   *PINE MOUNTAIN*

This ride is an out-and-back, 8.3-mile round-trip. It requires a moderate amount of strength and good bike handling skills. The first mile is an easy downhill on Pine Mountain Road. This section is a maintained, hard-packed dirt two-wheel-drive road in good condition. Going out and back on the single-track Trail 23W04 is more challenging. The condition of the trail is mixed, with some excellent firm surfaces, and some sandy and rocky sections. Back on Pine Mountain Road, you descend around the south side of Reyes Peak. This portion of the road is in poor condition and is very rocky in places. Finish with a moderately difficult, two-mile climb.

Pine Mountain is a long ridge that affords visitors a good look at the surrounding countryside. Beyond the forested hills and valleys to the south lie the beaches of Ventura and Oxnard. Trail 23W04 winds through a cool, shady conifer forest with intermittent views of the Cuyama Valley and Mt. Pinos. The roadside camping off of Pine Mountain Road is especially inviting, and is a great place to watch the city lights turn on.

General location: Begins at the end of the pavement on Pine Mountain Road (Forest Service Road 6N06), approximately 30 miles north of Ojai.
Elevation change: Starts at 7,000' and descends on Pine Mountain Road to an intersection with Trail 23W04 at 6,800'. You will gain elevation overall on Trail 23W04, with many ups and downs to the turnaround point. The return to Pine Mountain Road is mostly downhill with some short ascents. The ride along this trail adds an estimated 300' of elevation to the trip. Back on Pine Mountain Road you will drop from 6,800' to 6,400'. From this low point you have a short ride to the turnaround point at 6,450'. Returning, you will lose 50' before climbing again to an elevation of 7,000'. Total elevation gain: 950'.
Season: Late spring through early fall. The high elevation of this route makes for pleasant summer riding.
Services: No water is available on the ride or on Pine Mountain. Take all the water you will need with you. Water can be obtained at Ozena Ranger Station

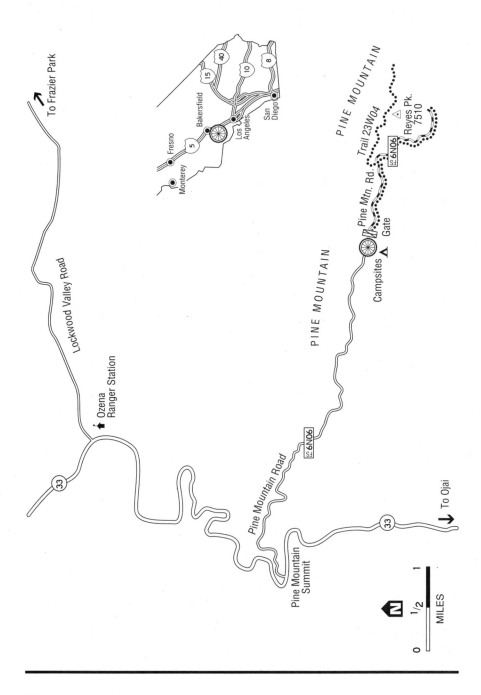

Haddock Mountain from Pine Mountain.

on CA 33; the station is located approximately 5 miles north of the intersection of Pine Mountain Road and CA 33. All services are available in Ojai. There is excellent car camping along Pine Mountain Road, but there are only some 12 sites.

Hazards: Cars are permitted on the first mile of the ride. Some sections of Trail 23W04 drop off sharply to the side and have been knocked down-slope. Walking your bike will help minimize further damage. You will encounter a washed-out section of road after turning off Trail 23W04 and descending on Pine Mountain Road. Walk your bike through. There is a lot of broken glass on Pine Mountain Road beyond this washed-out section.

Rescue index: Help is available in Ojai. A phone for emergency services can be found at the Wheeler Gorge Ranger Station, about 20 miles south of Pine Mountain Road on CA 33.

Land status: National forest.

Maps: USGS 7.5 minute quadrangle map: Reyes Peak.

Finding the trail: You can reach Pine Mountain Road (FS 6N06) by traveling north on CA 33 from US 101 in Ventura. Pine Mountain Road is not signed from the highway. Keep an eye on the milepost signs along the roadside as you drive north on CA 33. You come to Pine Mountain Summit (unmarked) near milepost sign 42.70. The paved Pine Mountain Road goes east from the summit. Pine Mountain Road climbs steeply and is narrow and twisting. Go slowly, watch for oncoming traffic, and sound your horn when approaching corners. The ride begins at a gate at the pavement's end, approximately 6 miles from CA 33. There is room to park a vehicle on the roadside near the gate. Additional parking can be found to the east along Pine Mountain Road.

Sources of additional information:

> Los Padres National Forest
> Ojai Ranger District
> 1190 E. Ojai Avenue
> Ojai, CA 93023
> (805) 646-4348

Notes on the trail: Leave the pavement at the gate on Pine Mountain Road. After 1 mile of riding you come to a turnaround area where the road seems to end. The road does continue, but is closed to most motor vehicles by means of some tank traps installed across the road. Turn left here onto unmarked Trail 23W04. The trail is not apparent from the road; look to the left (north) for a small dirt hill. Push your bike up the hill and you will see the trail. Stay left and uphill into the woods. After 1.5 miles on Trail 23W04 you will see some viewpoints on the right that you can walk to. Return the way you came. When you arrive back at Pine Mountain Road, turn left (go through the tank traps) and descend. You will reach the end of the road at a mound of earth. You can continue riding by pushing over the rise to an old road that will take you to a good vantage point. Return the way you came.

RIDE 10   *SESPE CREEK*

This out-and-back ride along Sespe Creek is easy to moderately difficult. It is an 8.5-mile round-trip on a dirt, four-wheel-drive road in mostly good condition. Some bike handling skills are needed as the route crosses through areas of loose rock and sand. You will also need to walk your bike over two dry creek beds in the first half mile of the ride.

The trail winds in and out of side canyons as it parallels the ridges above Sespe Creek. The rugged Topatopa Mountains can be seen in the distance to the southeast. Upon reaching the turnaround point at Bear Creek, you will find large boulders under shady cottonwoods and Matilja poppies nodding in the breeze. In all but the driest years the Sespe forms some shallow pools nearby, making this a nice spot for a cooling dip.

General location: Begins at the Lion Campground in the Rose Valley Recreation Area of the Los Padres National Forest, approximately 20 miles north of Ojai.
Elevation change: The ride starts at 3,165' and drops to a low point of 2,920'.

RIDE 10   *SESPE CREEK*

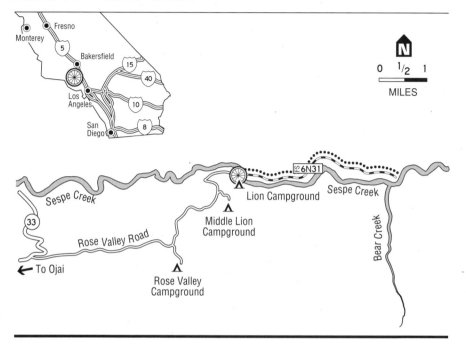

Rolling terrain along the course of the ride adds an estimated 200' of climbing to the trip. Total elevation gain: 445'.

Season: Spring and late fall are good times of the year for riding in the Rose Valley Recreation Area. The ride can be hot in the summer months and snow may fall in the winter.

Services: Water is available at Lion Campground. All services can be obtained in Ojai.

Hazards: The first mile or two may be busy with fishermen and hikers. Be courteous and control your speed. The trail narrows in places and drops off to the side.

Rescue index: Help can be found in Ojai.

Land status: National forest.

Maps: USGS 7.5 minute quadrangle maps: Lion Canyon and Topatopa Mountains.

Finding the trail: From Ojai, travel north on CA 33 approximately 13 miles to Rose Valley Road on the right. Take Rose Valley Road east and follow the signs to Lion Campground. Park regulations allow for the parking of vehicles at the day use parking area and they may be left overnight.

Topatopa Mountain from Sespe Creek Trail.

Sources of additional information:

Los Padres National Forest
Ojai Ranger District
1190 East Ojai Avenue
Ojai, CA 93023
(805) 646-4348

Notes on the trail: The trail heads east from the parking lot. Walk your bike down to and across Sespe Creek and climb a small hill. At the top of the hill you will find a sign for Forest Service Road 22W03 Piedra Blanca, Twin Forks, and Pine Mountain Lodge. Continue straight (east) to follow Sespe Creek. Ride 4 miles to a sandy, open area dotted with large boulders and cottonwoods. This is the turnaround point. Return the way you came.

RIDE 11 *CHIEF PEAK ROAD / NORDHOFF RIDGE*

This out-and-back, 14.6-mile round-trip ride is a challenge to all comers. The first 2.2 miles are a vicious ascent on paved Chief Peak Road. At times you will have difficulty keeping your front wheel on the ground. Staying on your bike will

RIDE 11 *CHIEF PEAK ROAD / NORDHOFF RIDGE*

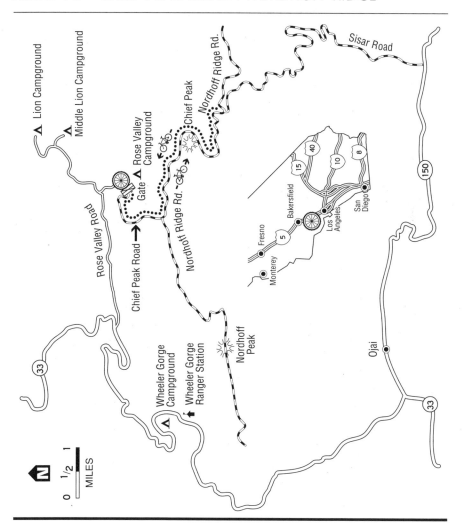

require a great deal of strength and determination; even walking your bike is a struggle! The level of difficulty moderates once you reach unpaved Nordhoff Ridge Road. Here you will traverse 1.5 miles of moderately difficult to strenuous terrain to Chief Peak. From this point, the riding is moderately difficult to the turnaround point at Sisar Road. Chief Peak Road is paved and in good condition with some gravel and a few potholes. Nordhoff Ridge Road is an unpaved, four-wheel-drive road in fair to good condition; some steep sections are rocky, rutted, and sandy.

Nordhoff Ridge view.

The views from the top of Nordhoff Ridge are outstanding. Look to the south for the beaches of Ventura and west for the Santa Ynez Mountains; to the east are the Topatopa Bluffs and the San Gabriel Mountains. To the north lies Piedra Blanca, Pine Mountain, and Rose Valley.

General location: Begins at the Rose Valley Campground in the Los Padres National Forest, approximately 20 miles north of Ojai.

Elevation change: The ride starts at 3,400' and climbs sharply to meet Nordhoff Ridge Road at 4,600'. A high point of 5,100' is attained at the intersection with Sisar Road. Undulations on the ridge add an estimated 1,000' of climbing to the ride. Total elevation gain: 2,700'.

Season: Due to the exposed nature of these roads, the best time to ride here is in the early spring or the late fall.

Services: Water is available at the Rose Valley Campground. All services can be obtained in Ojai.

Hazards: Cyclists must be proficient with all phases of bike handling skills to negotiate safely the roads described in this ride. Of greatest concern will be controlling your descent on Chief Peak Road. Keep your speed in check at all times; go slowly from the top. Watch for sand and gravel in the corners. Automobiles are permitted on the roads described in this ride.

Rescue index: Help can be found at the Wheeler Gorge Ranger Station on CA 33 (approximately 7 miles south of the intersection of CA 33 and Rose Valley Road), or in Ojai.

Land status: National forest.

Maps: USGS 7.5 minute quadrangle maps: Ojai, Lion Canyon, and Topatopa Mountains.

Finding the trail: From Ojai, travel north on CA 33 for approximately 15 miles to Rose Valley Road (Forest Service Road 6N31). Follow Rose Valley Road east for about 3 miles to a small lake on the left. Look for a road on the right that goes to the Rose Valley Falls and Campground. Turn right toward the falls and campground. You reach another small lake on the left just before the campground. Park next to the lake. The road that leads into Rose Valley Campground starts from this upper lake. Do not park in the campground unless you pay for a campsite.

Sources of additional information:

Los Padres National Forest
Ojai Ranger District
1190 East Ojai Avenue
Ojai, CA 93023
(805) 646-4348

Notes on the trail: Pedal up through Rose Valley Campground to a locked gate in the southwest corner of the campground. The ride begins at this gate that blocks off Chief Peak Road. Climb for 2.2 miles on Chief Peak Road to the pavement's end and turn left onto Nordhoff Ridge Road. After about 5 miles on Nordhoff Ridge Road, you will come to the turnaround point of the ride at a steel water tank and Sisar Road on the right. Return the way you came.

RIDE 12 *MT. PINOS LOOP*

This 21-mile loop (with out-and-back sections) is moderately difficult to strenuous, depending on your level of conditioning and acclimatization to the altitude. The trail conditions vary. One minute you are cycling along an excellent hard-packed dirt single-track trail; the next finds you dodging rocks on a degraded four-wheel-drive fire road. Some of the riding requires good bike handling skills. There are ten miles of cycling on good pavement.

A long paved climb allows you to enjoy some great descents on trails; climbing on the pavement is the easier way up. Terrific single-track riding and the views from the summit of Mt. Pinos highlight this ride.

General location: The ride begins at the McGill Campground on Mt. Pinos in the Los Padres National Forest (approximately 20 miles west of Interstate 5, midway between Los Angeles and Bakersfield).

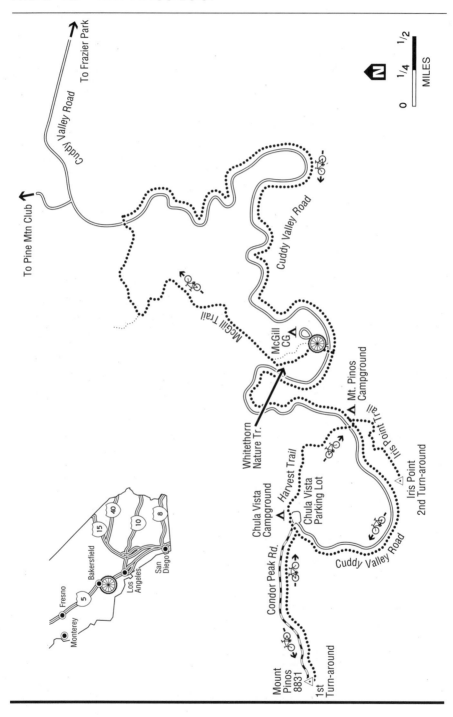

To Frazier Park

Cuddy Valley Road

To Pine Mtn Club

N

0   1/4   1/2

MILES

Cuddy Valley Road

McGill Trail

McGill CG

Mt. Pinos Campground

Whitethorn Nature Tr.

Iris Point Trail

Iris Point 2nd Turn-around

Chula Vista Campground

Harvest Trail

Chula Vista Parking Lot

Cuddy Valley Road

Condor Peak Rd.

Mount Pinos 8831

1st Turn-around

Fresno

Monterey

Bakersfield

15   40   10   8

5

Los Angeles

San Diego

McGill Trail single-track.

Elevation change: This tour starts at 7,830' at the McGill Campground. From the campground, climb on Whitethorn Nature Trail to 7,870' at the intersection with McGill Trail. Then drop to Cuddy Valley Road at 6,480'. Next, ascend on Cuddy Valley Road to the Chula Vista Parking Lot and the start of Condor Peak Road at 8,350'. Reach the summit of Mt. Pinos at 8,830'. Descend to Mt. Pinos Campground at 8,200', where you'll take Iris Point Trail to an overlook at 8,350'. It is downhill from the overlook to the entrance of the McGill Campground at 7,790'. Pedal up to your parked vehicle at 7,830'. Add an estimated 300' of climbing for rolling terrain encountered over the course of the ride. Total elevation gain: 2,880'.

Season: Late spring through early fall. Snow can be expected from December through April. Avoid busy weekends and holidays.

Services: Piped water can be obtained seasonally at McGill and Mt. Pinos Campgrounds. Services available in Frazier Park include gas, groceries, restaurant, drug store, and telephones. There are also limited services available in Lake of the Woods. The nearest lodging is in Gorman.

Hazards: Trails on Mt. Pinos are heavily used by hikers and other recreationists. Trails may narrow unexpectedly and contain hidden obstacles like tree roots, rocks, sand, and ruts. Expect traffic on the paved Cuddy Valley Road. Mountain weather is unpredictable; carry raingear.

Rescue index: Help can be found in Lake of the Woods, Frazier Park, and the Chuchupate Ranger Station (about 1 mile south of Cuddy Valley Road on Lockwood Valley Road in Lake of the Woods). The closest hospital is in Gorman.

Land status: National forest.

Maps: USGS 7.5 minute quadrangle maps: Sawmill Mountain and Cuddy Valley.

Finding the trail: From Los Angeles, follow I-5 approximately 85 miles north to the exit for Frazier Park and Frazier Mountain Road. This exit is 3 miles north of Gorman and 1.5 miles south of Lebec (near Tejon Pass). Follow Frazier Mountain Road west through the community of Frazier Park. Approximately 7 miles from I-5, in the small community of Lake of the Woods, Frazier Mountain Road becomes Cuddy Valley Road (at the intersection with Lockwood Valley Road). Continue straight (northwest) for another 5 miles where you come to a poorly marked intersection. A sign here points right to Pine Mountain Club. Stay left on Cuddy Valley Road as it veers south toward Mt. Pinos; do not go toward Pine Mountain Club. From this intersection you will drive approximately 5 miles of twisting mountain road to the entrance for the McGill Campground on the right. Enter the campground and stay to the right at the camping pay station. Here you will find a "hiker's" parking lot available for day use; no overnight parking is allowed.

Sources of additional information:

Los Padres National Forest Supervisor's Office
6144 Calle Real
Goleta, CA 93117
(805) 683-6711

Los Padres National Forest
Mt. Pinos Ranger District
Frazier Park, CA 93225
(805) 245-3731

24-Hour Taped Recreation Information
(805) 245-3449

Notes on the trail: The ride starts directly across from the fee pay station for campers using the McGill Campground. Here you will find the trailhead for

Whitethorn Nature Trail/McGill Trail. Bikes are permitted on the nature trail, but you may find it more enjoyable to walk and read the posted information. After .5 miles you come to a junction of trails at a bench. In front of you, 3 trails branch off. Take the trail to the right. You will pass a sign immediately on the right describing manzanita, and then reach another intersection where you pick up McGill Trail; stay straight as Whitethorn Nature Trail goes hard to the right. Travel 2 miles on McGill Trail to an unmarked intersection; stay right. Ride 1 more mile and arrive at Cuddy Valley Road. Turn right and climb on pavement for 8 miles to Chula Vista Parking Lot. At the parking lot, turn left onto Condor Peak Road. Stay left at intersections on Condor Peak Road to reach the summit of Mt. Pinos. On the way back from the summit you can go left to another viewpoint at some microwave towers.

Return down Condor Peak Road to Chula Vista Parking Lot. At the east end of the parking lot you will find a trail that takes you to the Chula Vista Campground. You will reach an intersection of trails on the outskirts of the campground. Continue straight (the trail to the left takes you to some pit toilets). A short distance beyond the campground you come to a couple of signs; one points right to Knoll Loop. The other directs you left onto Harvest Trail, but Harvest Trail is actually straight ahead. The trail is obvious as it goes downhill and is heavily gullied. Follow Harvest Trail for a little more than .5 miles to an intersection with a ski trail that goes right (west); continue straight to stay on Harvest Trail. Just beyond the intersection with the ski trail, you come to a "T" intersection. Turn right and ride about 100 yards to paved Cuddy Valley Road. Turn left and follow Cuddy Valley Road downhill to nearby Mt. Pinos Campground. Here you will find Iris Point Trail (a dirt fire road) on the right. The trail is partially blocked by piles of earth and is signed "Iris Point – 1 mile." Follow Iris Point Trail. Nearing Iris Point, you will come to an intersection; veer left to reach the viewpoint. Return the way you came from Iris Point to Cuddy Valley Road and turn right. It is about 2 miles down to the McGill Campground. Turn left into the campground to reach your parked vehicle.

Although the described ride is over 20 miles long, it could easily be broken into smaller loops or one-way rides. Families might enjoy a ride from their campsite at Mt. Pinos Campground to Iris Point and back. The outstanding views from the summit of Mt. Pinos can be experienced by making a 4-mile round-trip on Condor Peak Road from the Chula Vista Parking Lot. If you can arrange it, get dropped off at the Chula Vista Parking Lot, ride Harvest Trail, Cuddy Valley Road, and McGill Trail, and get picked up at the bottom. This eliminates the paved climb altogether!

RIDE 13 *LIEBRE MOUNTAIN*

A trip up Liebre Mountain on Forest Service Road 7N23 requires strong legs and a moderate amount of technical ability. It is an out-and-back, 14-mile round-trip. We recommend that you spend a few minutes warming up on the road you drive in on, the Old Ridge Route Road, before beginning the climb. The first one-half mile is very steep, and then the grade becomes moderately difficult to easy. After four miles of riding you reach gentle, rolling terrain that continues for about one mile. This is followed by a half-mile series of steep rocky ascents. After these hills, the cycling is moderately difficult as the road undulates to a viewpoint. The entire tour is on an unpaved, two-wheel-drive road in mostly good condition. Watch for ruts and loose material on the steeper portions of the route.

Splendid views abound as you climb up the west shoulder of Liebre Mountain. Emerging onto the ridge, you leave exposed, dry grasslands and roll into oak woodlands. Approximately seven miles from the start, expansive views open up to the east, south, and west. A good road, little traffic, and an excellent descent make climbing Liebre Mountain well worth the effort.

General location: Begins off of the Old Ridge Route Road in the northwest section of the Saugus District of the Angeles National Forest, approximately 65 miles northwest of Los Angeles.

Elevation change: FS 7N23 starts at 3,940' and reaches a high point of 5,680'. Another 200' of elevation is gained riding rolling terrain on the ridge. Total elevation gain: 1,940'.

Season: Early spring through late fall. Higher elevations make this a pleasant area for summer riding. Snow may close the road in the winter.

Services: There is no water on this ride. All services are available in the town of Gorman.

Hazards: Though traffic is generally light, vehicles are permitted on the road. Control your speed and watch for motorists on the return descent.

Rescue index: Help can be found in Gorman. This community is located off Interstate 5, about 15 miles west of the trailhead.

Land status: National forest.

Maps: USGS 7.5 minute quadrangle map: Liebre Mountain.

Finding the trail: From I-5, take the exit for CA 138/Quail Lake/Lancaster (about 6 miles south of Tejon Pass). Proceed east on CA 138/Lancaster Road for 4.2 miles to an intersection where CA 138/Lancaster Road goes left and Pine Canyon Road/N2 goes straight. Continue straight on Pine Canyon Road/N2. Follow Pine Canyon Road/N2 for 2 miles in a southerly direction to the Old Ridge Route Road on the right. Turn right onto the Old Ridge Route Road. This road climbs through Sandberg (just a few buildings) and soon deteriorates to

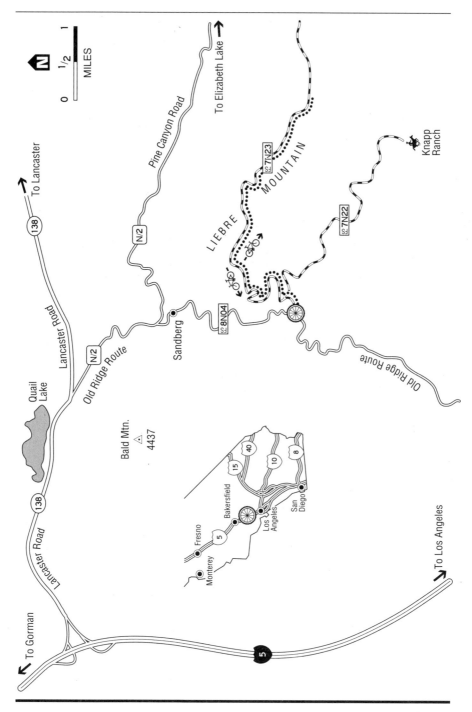

Road up the shoulder of Liebre Mountain.

broken pavement. About 3 miles beyond Sandberg, you will come to FS 7N23 on the left. It is marked by a sign: "Castaic 25 miles, Bear Campground 9 miles, Sawmill Campground 14 miles." Park here on the side of the Old Ridge Route Road at a dirt pullout area on the right; overnight parking is permitted.

Sources of additional information:

Angeles National Forest
Saugus Ranger District
30800 Bouquet Canyon Road
Saugus, CA 91350
(805) 296-9710

Notes on the trail: Follow FS 7N23 (marked by the sign for Castaic, Bear Campground, and Sawmill Campground). You will come to an unmarked intersection after .5 miles. Stay left and uphill (the road to the right goes to Knapp Ranch). Stay on the main road as many side roads branch off near the top of Liebre Mountain. You will reach a viewpoint after riding approximately 7 miles. Turn around and return the way you came.

RIDE 14 *BURNT PEAK / UPPER SHAKE*

This out-and-back, 14-mile round-trip is recommended for strong cyclists and determined intermediates. The entire circuit is on unpaved four-wheel-drive roads in fair to good condition. The first two miles climb moderately on Forest Service Road 7N23. This is followed by a relentlessly steep and fairly technical one-mile ascent on FS 7N23A. The next mile brings some relief as the road descends and then rolls up and down moderately. From here the route climbs sharply for two miles to the summit of Burnt Peak. The steep sections of FS 7N23A contain some washboarding, loose rocks, and ruts.

The predominant vistas on the way to Burnt Peak are of the Antelope Valley and the Tehachapi Mountains. Once on top, you obtain a panoramic view of the surrounding countryside. On the return from the peak you take a side trip to the Upper Shake Campground. This is a cool, quiet spot with large shade trees and picnic tables.

General location: Begins at the intersection of FS 7N23 and Pine Canyon Road, 4.3 miles west of Lake Hughes in the Saugus District of the Angeles National Forest, approximately 80 miles north of downtown Los Angeles.

Elevation change: The ride starts at 4,265' and climbs to a high point of 5,790' atop Burnt Peak. On the return you drop to 4,465' at the Upper Shake Campground. From the campground you climb to 4,665' and then descend to 4,265' at Pine Canyon Road. Total elevation gain: 1,725'.

Season: Early spring through late fall. It may be cooler and windy at the crest of Burnt Peak; be prepared with warm clothing. Weekend and holiday traffic can be heavy.

Services: There is no water on this ride. All services can be found in the town of Lake Hughes.

Hazards: The roads described in this ride access public campgrounds and see a fair amount of vehicular traffic. Be careful when approaching blind corners.

Rescue index: Help is available in the town of Lake Hughes.

Land status: National forest.

Maps: USGS 7.5 minute quadrangle map: Burnt Peak.

Finding the trail: The route begins at FS 7N23 and Pine Canyon Road. From downtown Los Angeles, follow Interstate 5 north for approximately 60 miles to the exit for CA 138/Quail Lake/Lancaster. From points north, take I-5 south 6 miles beyond Tejon Pass to the exit for CA 138/Quail Lake/Lancaster. Proceed east on CA 138/Lancaster Road for 4.2 miles, to an intersection where CA 138/Lancaster Road goes left and Pine Canyon Road/N2 goes straight. Continue straight on Pine Canyon Road/N2 toward Lake Hughes and Elizabeth Lake. After approximately 15 miles you come to a sign on the right that reads "Upper

RIDE 14 *BURNT PEAK / UPPER SHAKE*

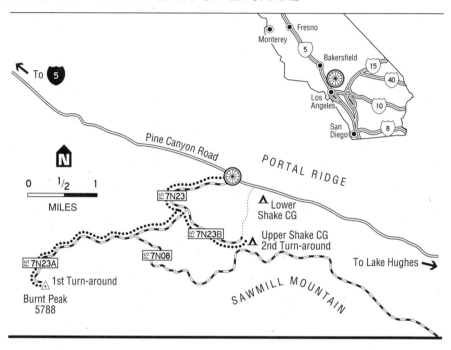

Shake 3 miles, Sawmill Campground 5 miles, Burnt Peak 7 miles." This is the start of FS 7N23. Park in the pullout at the beginning of the road; cars may be left overnight.

Sources of additional information:

> Angeles National Forest
> Saugus Ranger District
> 30800 Bouquet Canyon Road
> Saugus, CA 91350
> (805) 296-9710

Notes on the trail: Follow FS 7N23 for 2 miles to the intersection with FS 7N23B and FS 7N23A; turn right onto FS 7N23A toward Burnt Peak. Continue straight at the sign reading "Burnt Peak 3 Miles." Reach the ride's first turnaround point at the Burnt Peak microwave towers. Return the way you came. At the intersection with FS 7N23 and FS 7N23B, turn right onto FS 7N23B and follow it to the Upper Shake Campground. The Upper Shake Campground is the ride's second turnaround point. Return the way you came.

RIDE 15 *GRASS MOUNTAIN / SOUTH PORTAL CANYON*

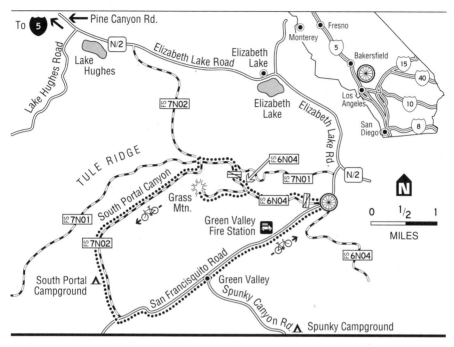

RIDE 15 *GRASS MOUNTAIN / SOUTH PORTAL CANYON*

This is a 13.2-mile ride. It consists of an out-and-back spur to Grass Mountain and a loop through South Portal Canyon. It is an appropriate trip for intermediate cyclists with good bike handling skills. The climb up Grass Mountain is moderately steep. It is mostly downhill from the top of the peak to the paved San Francisquito Canyon Road. Complete the circuit with four miles of uphill riding on San Francisquito Canyon Road; it is easy at first, and then becomes increasingly difficult as you near your vehicle. The dirt roads followed on this ride are generally in good condition. There is sand and some ruts where these roads get steeper.

From the summit of Grass Mountain you get a good view of the surrounding area. Portal Ridge and Elizabeth Lake lie to the north. Beyond these landmarks are the arid Antelope Valley and the Tehachapi Mountains. The peaks of the distant San Gabriel Mountains are prominent on the eastern horizon. To the south

South Portal Canyon.

are Jupiter Mountain and the community of Green Valley. The ride through South Portal Canyon is one of the finest fire road descents in the Angeles National Forest.

General location: The trip starts on Forest Service Road 6N04 off San Francisquito Canyon Road, 3 miles south of the community of Elizabeth Lake, approximately 30 miles northeast of Valencia.

Elevation change: Begins near 3,770′ and climbs to a high point of 4,605′ at the top of Grass Mountain. The route descends to a low point of 2,600′ at the intersection of FS 7N02 and San Francisquito Canyon Road. Pedal uphill on San Francisquito Canyon Road to return to the trailhead at 3,770′. Rolling terrain adds an estimated 100′ of climbing to the ride. Total elevation gain: 2,105′.

Season: Spring through late fall. Winter snows are common and summers are generally hot and dry.

Services: No water is available on the ride. Patrons can often obtain water from friendly store proprietors. The nearby communities of Green Valley, Elizabeth Lake, and Lake Hughes offer camping, groceries, and gasoline. All services are available in Valencia.

Hazards: Approach all descents with caution; some sections of road may be sandy or contain loose rocks and/or ruts. Control your speed and anticipate trail users approaching in the opposite direction. Paved San Francisquito Canyon Road is a secondary highway that sees heaviest use on summer weekends and holidays; there is no shoulder.

Rescue index: Help can be found at the Green Valley Fire Station (on San Francisquito Canyon Road, about 1 mile south of the start of the ride) or in the community of Elizabeth Lake.

Land status: National forest.

Maps: USGS 7.5 minute quadrangle map: Lake Hughes.

Finding the trail: From Los Angeles, follow Interstate 5 north. Drive about 10 miles beyond the I-5/I-210 interchange to the exit for Six Flags/Magic Mountain. Proceed east on Magic Mountain Road for 2.5 miles and turn left onto Bouquet Canyon Road (CA 126) in the community of Saugus. Follow Bouquet Canyon Road north for approximately 18 miles and turn left on Spunky Canyon Road. Follow Spunky Canyon Road for 4 miles to the intersection with San Francisquito Canyon Road. Turn right onto San Francisquito Canyon Road and follow it for about 1 mile to the top of the hill where a sign reads "Grass Mountain, South Portal, Tule Ridge." Park on the east side of San Francisquito Canyon Road at the intersection with FS 6N04. Do not block access to FS 6N04.

Sources of additional information:

Angeles National Forest
Saugus Ranger District
30800 Bouquet Canyon Road
Saugus, CA 91350
(805) 296-9710

Notes on the trail: Follow FS 6N04 west toward Grass Mountain (a sign points the way). A short distance up FS 6N04, at an intersection of roads, take the middle road that has a gate across it. About 1.5 miles beyond the gate, FS 6N04 intersects with an unmarked spur road to Grass Mountain. Stay left and follow the spur road to the summit. From the top of Grass Mountain, return the way you came to the last intersection. Turn left here, back onto unsigned FS 6N04. From this intersection it is .7 miles to a gate. Walk your bike around it. Just beyond the gate is an unmarked intersection. This is the western terminus of FS 6N04. Stay to the left (westerly) on the main road; you are now on FS 7N01. A short distance on FS 7N01 brings you to an intersection of several unmarked roads and trails. From here you have a good view of FS 7N02 as it heads down into South Portal Canyon. Turn to the left to descend on FS 7N02 (there are a couple of trails that also go left here; stay on the fire road). You will pass the South Portal Campground after about 4 miles on FS 7N02. You will arrive at San Francisquito Canyon Road .8 miles beyond the campground. Turn left onto San Francisquito Canyon Road and proceed uphill for 4 miles to your parked vehicle.

RIDE 16 *SIERRA PELONA / FOREST SERVICE ROAD 6N08*

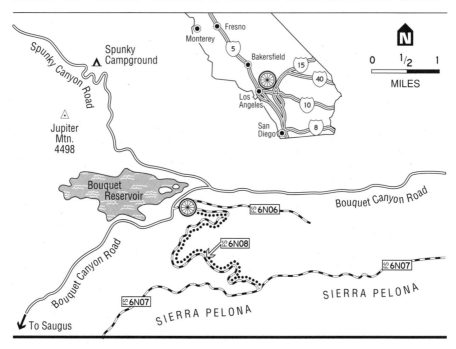

RIDE 16 *SIERRA PELONA / FOREST SERVICE ROAD 6N08*

This out-and-back, 9.4-mile round-trip ride is suited to intermediate cyclists. The climb is moderately difficult with some steep sections, but it is not too arduous or technically demanding. Forest Service Road 6N08 is a two-wheel-drive hard-packed dirt road in good condition. There are loose rocks and minor ruts on steeper portions of the road.

The scenery is not particularly outstanding, but the views from the crest of the Sierra Pelona are nice. The Sierra Pelona Valley, Soledad Canyon, Parker Mountain, and Magic Mountain are prominent from this vantage point. The mostly downhill return to your vehicle is fast and fun.

General location: Begins near the Bouquet Reservoir off Bouquet Canyon Road in the Saugus District of the Angeles National Forest, approximately 25 miles northeast of Valencia.

Elevation change: The ride starts at approximately 3,550′, descends to 3,400′

Matilja poppies in bloom atop the Sierra Pelona.

in the first .8 miles, and then climbs to 4,750' at the turnaround point. Total elevation gain: 1,500'.

Season: Early spring through late fall. Spring brings good wildflower displays and bothersome flies. Plan for an early start during the hottest months.

Services: No potable water is available on this ride. The nearest water source is at the U.S. Forest Service Spunky Campground. To find this campground, drive north on Bouquet Canyon Road from the intersection of Bouquet Canyon Road and FS 6N08. After .5 miles turn left on Spunky Canyon Road. Follow Spunky Canyon Road for 3 miles to the campground on the right. All services can be obtained in Saugus.

Hazards: Stay alert for other trail users, especially motorized all-terrain-vehicles. It is busy here on summer weekends and holidays. Control your speed on the descent.

Rescue index: Help is available at the Saugus District Ranger Station on Bouquet Canyon Road (approximately 8 miles north of Saugus and approximately 9 miles south of the start of the ride).

Land status: National forest.

Maps: USGS 7.5 minute quadrangle map: Sleepy Valley.

Finding the trail: From Los Angeles, follow Interstate 5 north. Drive about 10 miles beyond the I-5/I-210 interchange to the exit for Six Flags/Magic Mountain. Proceed east on Magic Mountain Road for 2.5 miles and turn left on Bouquet

Canyon Road (CA 126) in the community of Saugus. Follow Bouquet Canyon Road north for approximately 17 miles to Bouquet Reservoir. FS 6N08 is unmarked but is easy to find. FS 6N08 goes east from Bouquet Canyon Road just north of milepost 7.19. If you reach the intersection of Bouquet Canyon Road and Spunky Canyon Road, you have gone too far north by .5 miles. Once you locate FS 6N08, follow it east. After .3 miles, you will come to the intersection of FS 6N08 and FS 6N06. Park at the roadside at this intersection. Do not block access to the roads.

Sources of additional information:

Angeles National Forest
Saugus Ranger District
30800 Bouquet Canyon Road
Saugus, CA 91350
(805) 296-9710

Notes on the trail: From the parking area at the intersection of FS 6N08 and FS 6N06, follow FS 6N08 as it proceeds downhill. Continue on FS 6N08 as it turns hard to the right and begins to climb. Pass Artesian Spring Trail on the left after 2 miles of riding. Soon after you will pass Artesian Spring on the right. Two miles beyond the spring you will reach an intersection; turn left. It is .6 miles from the last intersection to the crest of the Sierra Pelona at a "T" intersection. Turn around and return the way you came.

RIDE 17   *BIG SYCAMORE CANYON / POINT MUGU STATE PARK*

Contained within Point Mugu State Park are mountain bike routes suited to all abilities. Strength and good bike handling skills are required of cyclists following this 15.5-mile loop. The first 5.6 miles are a gentle ascent on Big Sycamore Canyon Trail to Ranch Center Road. The pedaling on Ranch Center Road is moderately difficult for 1.5 miles, and then the road drops rapidly for .8 miles. Wood Canyon Trail is picked up at this point and the route continues downhill for two miles to Overlook Trail at Deer Camp Junction. On Overlook Trail you climb very steeply for 1.5 miles and tackle the aptly named Hell Hill. The biking then gets easier as you ride around the south side of an unnamed peak. The loop ends with an exhilarating three-mile descent.

The first 4.5 miles are over an unpaved, two-wheel-drive road in good condition. This is followed by 3.2 miles of pavement. The remaining miles are on dirt trails in fair to good condition with some loose gravel and sand.

This ride has it all: an easy warm-up, lovely scenery, tree-shaded lanes, open

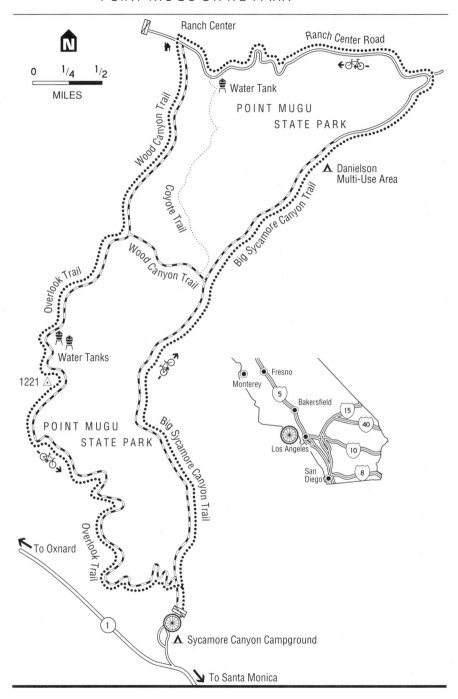

N

0 1/4 1/2
MILES

Ranch Center

Ranch Center Road

Wood Canyon Trail

Water Tank

POINT MUGU
STATE PARK

Coyote Trail

Danielson
Multi-Use Area

Big Sycamore Canyon Trail

Overlook Trail

Wood Canyon Trail

Water Tanks

1221

Monterey
Fresno
5
Bakersfield
15
40
10
Los Angeles
8
San Diego

POINT MUGU
STATE PARK

Big Sycamore Canyon Trail

To Oxnard

Overlook Trail

1

Sycamore Canyon Campground

To Santa Monica

Easy riding in Big Sycamore Canyon.

roads, single-track trails, a grinding "sweat-in-the-eyes" climb, exhilarating descents, splendid coastal views, ample water, wildlife, and wildflowers. Who could ask for more?

General location: Starts at the campground in Big Sycamore Canyon at Point Mugu State Park (approximately 30 miles west of Los Angeles).

Elevation change: Big Sycamore Canyon Trail begins at 25' of elevation and climbs to 400' at Ranch Center Road. On Ranch Center Road you climb to 700', and then drop to 500' at the intersection with Wood Canyon Trail. You will then descend on Wood Canyon Trail to Deer Camp Junction at 300', and climb to 1,200' on Overlook Trail before descending to the trailhead. Total elevation gain: 1,575'.

Season: Can be enjoyed year-round. Due to its beautiful trails and proximity to a large urban area, Point Mugu State Park is a popular riding area. Good bets for light-use times are weekday mornings. Trail closure due to high fire danger can occur at any time. Call the district ranger for current conditions.

Services: You will find water at the Big Sycamore Canyon Campground and at various locations along the ride. The last place to fill up before climbing on Overlook Trail is at the Ranch Center Maintenance Center. All services are available in Malibu.

Hazards: The park is well used by cyclists, equestrians, hikers, and runners.

Care must be taken to watch out for others on the trails. Be especially cautious around blind corners. Watch for motor vehicles on Ranch Center Road.

Rescue index: Help can be obtained at the park headquarters located at the park's entrance. There is a pay phone here as well.

Land status: State park.

Maps: A park map can be purchased at the headquarters. It is an excellent guide to this trail.

Finding the trail: The trail begins at the north end of the Big Sycamore Canyon Campground in Point Mugu State Park. The park's entrance is off the Pacific Coast Highway (CA 1), 32 miles west of Santa Monica and 12 miles east of Oxnard. There is a day-use fee for parking at the campground or across the highway at the beach. Automobiles may also be parked outside the park in an area off the highway marked "No Parking 10 p.m. to 5 a.m."

Sources of additional information:

Department of Parks and Recreation
Santa Monica Mountains District
2860A Camino Dos Rios
(818) 706-1310 or (805) 987-3303

Department of Parks and Recreation
State of California - the Resources Agency
P.O. Box 2390
Sacramento, CA 95811

24-hour recorded message for Santa Monica Mountains fire conditions:
(213) 454-2372.

Notes on the trail: Follow Big Sycamore Canyon Trail. The road turns to pavement and climbs to an intersection with Ranch Center Road. Turn left and follow Ranch Center Road to Ranch Center and Wood Canyon Trail on the left. Take Wood Canyon Trail to Deer Camp Junction. Continue straight onto Overlook Trail as Wood Canyon Trail veers left. Follow Overlook Trail to Big Sycamore Canyon Trail and turn right to return to the trailhead.

Cyclists have damaged portions of the park's trails by skidding their tires. Walk your bike if you cannot descend without skidding.

Bicycles are not permitted on all of the trails in the park. Obey signs indicating closings.

RIDE 18   *CHARMLEE PARK*

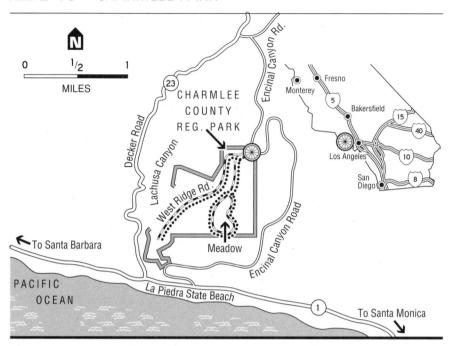

RIDE 18   *CHARMLEE PARK*

Ride an easier loop around the park's meadow or choose a demanding out-and-back trip on West Ridge Road. Combine the two for up to eight miles of pedaling. The trails in the meadow are hard-packed dirt in good condition with several eroded, short, steep hills. West Ridge Road is hard-packed dirt in fair condition. Motor vehicles are not allowed in the park.

Here is a place where beginners can tone their muscles and work on their bike handling technique. Families can enjoy riding these trails together. West Ridge Road offers intermediate riders a challenge and a chance to improve their skills.

Charmlee Park is well known for its abundant wildflowers; they are most prolific in the meadow. To the south are excellent views of the Santa Monica Mountains, Catalina, and the Channel Islands.

General location: Charmlee Park is located off Encinal Canyon Road, approximately 30 miles west of Santa Monica.

Elevation change: Riding out and back on West Ridge Road involves an esti-

A view from the top of Charmlee Ridge.

mated 400′ of climbing. Hills in the meadow and on other roads in the park can add an additional 200′ of climbing to the ride. Total elevation gain: 600′.

Season: This popular spot is open year-round and is often crowded on summer weekends. It is lovely in the spring when wildflowers fill the meadows and hillsides. Cold temperatures, rain, and fog can be expected in the winter.

Services: Water and restrooms are available at the park. All services can be obtained in Malibu.

Hazards: Portions of Charmlee Park's trails are rutted, sandy, and rocky. Watch for other recreationists and control your speed.

Rescue index: Help can be found in Malibu. Emergency assistance may be summoned at a pay phone at La Piedra State Beach, at the intersection of Encinal Canyon Road and the Pacific Coast Highway (CA 1).

Land status: County park.

Maps: A trail map may be purchased by writing to the park.

Finding the trail: Follow the Pacific Coast Highway (CA 1) to Encinal Canyon Road. Encinal Canyon Road is located about 20 miles east of Oxnard and about 30 miles west of Santa Barbara. Travel north on Encinal Canyon Road for 4.5 miles to the park entrance on the left. There is a small dirt parking lot on the right as you enter.

Sources of additional information:

Charmlee Natural Area Park
P.O. Box 1151
Agoura, CA 91301
(213) 457-7247

Notes on the trail: From the parking area, walk your bike around the locked gate and enter the park. Ahead and to the left is a live oak-shaded picnic area and the trailhead. Stay left on the trails to reach the meadow. Stay to the right to reach West Ridge Road.

RIDE 19 ZUMA RIDGE

This is a very difficult 13.6-mile loop. The ride begins with a moderately steep 2.7-mile ascent up Zuma Ridge Motorway. This is followed by a sharp two-mile descent into Zuma Canyon on Edison Road. Get your feet wet crossing a stream before beginning a tough two-mile climb out of the canyon. So far, the ride has followed four-wheel-drive fire roads in poor to fair condition. The steepest sections of these roads are rock strewn and sandy; negotiating them will require good bike handling skills. Descend on Kanan-Dume Road (two-lane, paved) to mostly level CA 1 (four-lane, paved). Pedal up moderately steep Busch Drive (two-lane paved) to complete the trip.

Advanced riders will appreciate the varied terrain and solitude that this ride offers. Expansive views call out for your attention as you are forced to concentrate on the climb at hand. Stop for a moment to look at Santa Monica Bay and the enormous City of Los Angeles to the east. Catalina Island sits on the horizon to the south, and directly below you are long sandy beaches and the shimmering Pacific. Zuma Canyon's red rock walls are an impressive sight as they tower above the switchbacking trail. Need some incentive to get yourself going again? How about a cool dip in the ocean at Zuma Beach? Onward!

General location: Starts at the north end of Busch Drive. Busch Drive is off CA 1, approximately 20 miles west of Santa Monica.

RIDE 19 *ZUMA RIDGE*

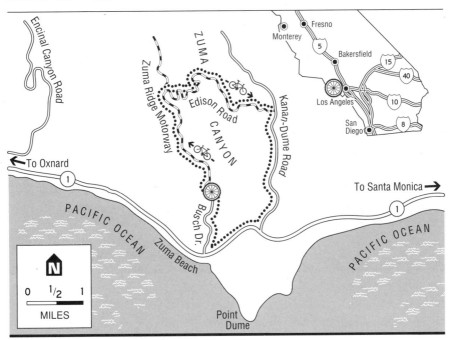

Elevation change: The loop begins at 325' of elevation and climbs to 1,640' on Zuma Ridge Motorway. You will lose 1,000' riding from the ridge to the bottom of Zuma Canyon. This is followed by a 1,000' climb back out of the canyon and then a descent to sea level. End with 325' of climbing to the trailhead. Total elevation gain: 2,640'.

Season: You can ride here any time of the year. Dry conditions, steep slopes, and dense vegetation make wildfires a threat from the spring through the fall. Call (213) 454-2372 for 24-hour recorded information on the Santa Monica Mountains' fire conditions and closures. Winters see an increase in precipitation and fog.

Services: No water is available on the ride. All services can be found in Malibu.

Hazards: This area is used heavily by equestrians. The descent on Edison Road is very steep and is dotted with rocks. The paved downhill on Kanan-Dume Road is steep, but the road is wide and traffic passes easily. There is a wide shoulder on CA 1.

Rescue index: Help can be obtained in Malibu or at the State Beaches along CA 1.

Land status: National recreation area.

Zuma Ridge Motorway and Edison Road.

Maps: A good trail map of the Santa Monica Mountains may be purchased from the Coastal Trails Foundation, P.O. Box 20073, Santa Barbara, CA 93120.

Finding the trail: The ride begins at the end of Busch Drive. Busch Drive meets CA 1 across from Zuma Beach at the west end of Malibu. From the west, follow CA 1 east of Oxnard for approximately 25 miles to Busch Drive on the left. From the east, follow CA 1 west of Santa Monica for about 20 miles to Busch Drive on the right. Turn north onto Busch Drive and follow it for 1.4 miles to a parking area where the road turns to dirt; this is the beginning of Zuma Ridge Motorway.

Sources of additional information:

National Park Service
Santa Monica Mountains Recreation Area
30401 Agoura
Agoura Hills, CA 91301
(818) 597-9192

Notes on the trail: From the parking area, face the water tower. The two roads in front of you both enter the motorway. Take the one to the left; it is less steep. After 2.7 miles on Zuma Ridge Motorway, the road crests at some electric towers and meets Edison Road. Turn right before the towers onto unsigned Edison Road. Stay on Edison Road for the remaining unpaved miles. Upon reaching paved Kanan-Dume Road, turn right and follow it downhill to CA 1. Turn right onto CA 1 and ride 1 mile to Busch Drive on the right. Climb on Busch Drive to your parked vehicle.

RIDE 20 *CRAGS ROAD*

Crags Road is a delightfully easy, out-and-back, 7.8-mile round-trip ride. It travels over mostly flat terrain and is recommended for beginning mountain bikers. There are a few short hills. Most of the ride is on good, hard-packed dirt roads. Expect some short stretches of sand and light washboarding.

On this trip you cross over several bridges as the road follows the meandering Malibu Creek. Bordering the creek are large sycamores. Huge oaks shade picnic tables at the Visitor Center. The rugged peaks of Goat Buttes lie to the south and are prominent over much of the ride. Water-oriented birds abound and fishermen enjoy good bass fishing in Century Lake.

A mile beyond the lake you will find a rusted jeep and an ambulance next to the trail. This is the former set of the television series "M.A.S.H." Prior to the land's incarnation as Malibu Creek State Park, it belonged to 20th Century Fox. Several "Tarzan" movies, many westerns, and "Planet Of The Apes" were filmed here.

General location: Malibu Creek State Park is 6 miles north of Malibu on Las Virgines/Malibu Canyon Road.
Elevation change: You begin riding at 500′ and follow the creek upstream to 700′. Rolling terrain adds an estimated 100′ of climbing to the route. Total elevation gain: 300′.
Season: Open year-round. This is a very popular park on summer weekends and holidays.
Services: Water, restrooms, and camping are available at Malibu Creek State Park. All services can be obtained in Malibu.
Hazards: These trails are often busy. Ride slowly and watch for others as you approach corners.
Rescue index: Help can be found in Malibu. Emergency assistance may be available at the Visitor Center or at the entry kiosk off Las Virgines/Malibu Canyon Road.
Land status: State park.
Maps: A trail map may be purchased at the entry kiosk or at the Visitor Center.
Finding the trail: The park entrance is just south of Mulholland Highway on Las Virgines/Malibu Canyon Road. From the Pacific Coast Highway (CA 1) in Malibu, drive north for 6 miles on Las Virgines/Malibu Canyon Road to the park entrance on the left. From the north, follow US 101 to Las Virgines/Malibu

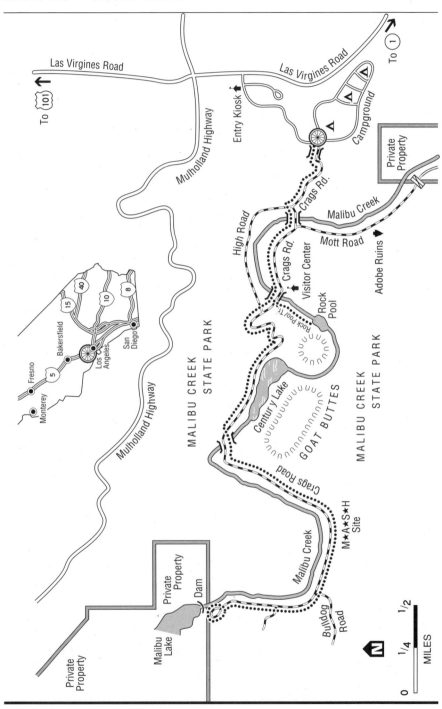

Malibu Creek on Crags Road.

Canyon Road. Go south on Las Virgines/Malibu Canyon Road for 3 miles to Mulholland Highway. Continue past Mulholland Highway for .3 miles to the park entrance on the right. Pay a day-use fee at the entry kiosk and proceed south to the furthest parking area.

Sources of additional information:

Department of Parks and Recreation
Santa Monica Mountains District
2860A Camino Dos Rios

Newbury Park, CA 91320
(818) 706-1310

Park Information: (805) 499-2112

24-hour recorded message for Santa Monica Mountains' fire conditions:
(213) 454-2372.

Notes on the trail: From the parking area, continue south on the park's entrance road to a road on the right signed "Authorized Vehicles Only." This is the beginning of Crags Road. Follow Crags Road and stay left at the first intersection to cross the river on a large concrete bridge. Turn right immediately after the bridge toward the Visitor Center (a left turn takes you down Mott Road to some adobe ruins). Past the Visitor Center and across another bridge you will find the signed Rock Pool Trail on the left. Take it for a short trip to the pools. Return to Crags Road and turn left. Climb over the biggest hill of the ride to a signed road for Century Lake on the left. Continue straight. You will reach the "M.A.S.H." site after about 3 miles of cycling. After passing the "M.A.S.H." site, stay right at the next 2 intersections to reach the dam at Malibu Lake. Return the way you came.

The Visitor Center has outstanding exhibits describing the natural and social histories of the park. It is open on weekends and holidays from noon to 4 P.M.

RIDE 21 *EAGLE ROCK / EAGLE SPRINGS*

This out-and-back, six-mile round-trip ride (with a loop to Eagle Rock) is moderately difficult. Begin with 3.5 miles of moderately steep climbing, interspersed with some steep uphills, level stretches, and rolling terrain. There is a "screamer" descent just before reaching Eagle Rock. It is mostly downhill riding on the return. The route follows four-wheel-drive dirt fire roads in fair to good condition. Some of the steeper sections contain loose rocks and sand. Riding here requires good bike handling skills.

The view from Eagle Rock is excellent. The canyons and ridges of Topanga State Park stretch out below you. In the distance are Santa Ynez, the San Fernando Valley, and the Pacific Ocean. After your ride, lock your bike and take some time to walk the one-mile self-guided nature trail at Trippet Ranch.

General location: Begins at Trippet Ranch in Topanga State Park, approximately 10 miles northwest of Santa Monica.
Elevation change: Starts at 1,310' and climbs for 1 mile to 1,700'. From here it drops to the Eagle Rock/Eagle Springs intersection at 1,600', and then climbs

RIDE 21   *EAGLE ROCK / EAGLE SPRINGS*

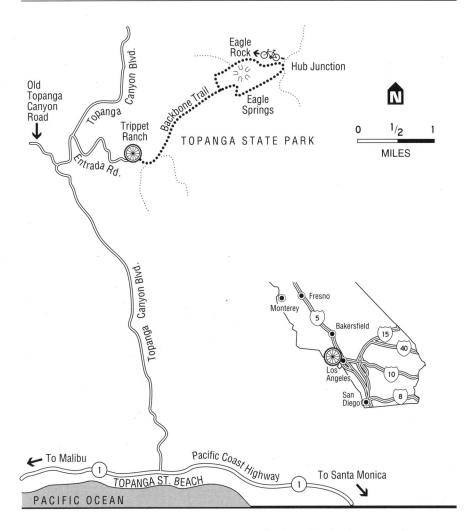

to the Hub intersection at 2,000′. You reach the ride's high point of 2,100′ at Eagle Rock. Total elevation gain: 890′.

Season: This route can be ridden year-round. The best seasons are the early spring and late fall; temperatures are cooler, the vegetation is greener, and there are fewer hikers using the trails.

Services: Water can be obtained at the restrooms near the Trippet Ranch parking area. All services are available in the community of Topanga.

Eagle Rock.

Hazards: Topanga State Park is popular with equestrians, hikers, and cyclists. Rattlesnakes reside in the park. If you encounter one, let him avoid you; they will not attack unless disturbed.

Rescue index: The nearest help in an emergency is available at Trippet Ranch or in the community of Topanga. The closest public phone is at Trippet Ranch, in the breezeway near the office.

Land status: State park.

Maps: A map of Topanga State Park may be obtained at the Trippet Ranch Information Center. It is a good guide to this trail.

Finding the trail: The ride begins at the trailhead in the southeast corner of the day-use parking lot at Trippet Ranch in Topanga State Park. From Santa

Monica, follow CA 1 west for approximately 6 miles to Topanga Canyon Boulevard (Topanga Canyon Boulevard intersects with CA 1 across from Topanga State Beach). Follow Topanga Canyon Boulevard north for approximately 5 miles to Entrada Road. Turn right (east) onto Entrada Road. Stay left at all intersections to reach the Trippet Ranch day-use parking area. Paid parking is available. Hours of operation are from 8 A.M. to 7 P.M. in the summer and 8 A.M. to 5 P.M. in the winter.

Sources of additional information:

> Department of Parks and Recreation
> Santa Monica Mountains District
> 2860A Camino Dos Rios
> Newbury Park, CA 91320
> (818) 706-1310

Notes on the trail: Start at the trailhead in the southeast corner of the parking lot. Follow the fire road for .2 miles to a junction of roads with a sign for Eagle Rock and other trails. Turn left toward Eagle Rock and proceed to the intersection with a sign for Eagle Rock and Eagle Spring. Turn right toward Eagle Spring and follow the road to the Hub intersection. At the Hub intersection, turn hard to the left and ride uphill. Take this fire road to the sign for North Loop Trail/ Eagle Rock. Continue on the main road to Eagle Rock. Go .5 miles beyond Eagle Rock to the intersection for Eagle Spring. Continue straight to return the way you came.

Some trails may be temporarily closed due to high fire danger during dry periods. Call (213) 454-2372 for a 24-hour recorded message for Santa Monica Mountains fire conditions.

RIDE 22 *INSPIRATION POINT*

This is a moderately difficult to strenuous loop with some one-way spurs. The ride is 13.7 miles long. The first 2.5 miles are a tough ascent on paved Forest Service Road 2N50. From here the climbing moderates in difficulty and the route changes to a two-wheel-drive dirt road. The road was built originally for electric streetcars, but they could not surmount a grade steeper than 7 percent. This dirt portion of FS 2N50 allows for good traction with only short stretches of sand, loose rocks, and rutting. The descent on the single-track Sam Merrill Trail to Echo Mountain requires a high degree of technical skill, as does the return to FS 2N50 on Echo Mountain Trail. These trails hug canyon walls, are extremely narrow, and contain steep switchbacks. Sheer drop-offs are common. Sections of these single-tracks are rutted, sandy, and present obstacles like old

RIDE 22 *INSPIRATION POINT*

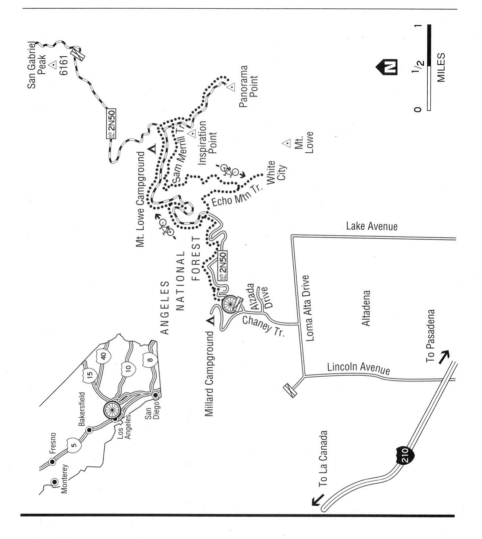

railroad ties, exposed tree roots, and rocks. Some segments of the trails have been "knocked down" into the canyon. Carrying your bike over these degraded areas will minimize further damage and help assure you a safe passage.

After 1.8 miles of riding, you come across the first of several interpretive displays depicting aspects of a once popular tourist attraction that was located here. In 1893, entrepreneur Thaddeus Lowe opened his Mount Lowe Railway. It employed a steep incline railroad and trolleys to bring sightseers into the San

Horseshoe Curve and Millard Canyon.

Gabriel Mountains. Also of interest are sighting tubes at Inspiration Point that aid in identifying distant landmarks.

General location: The route starts at the end of Chaney Trail above Altadena, approximately 15 miles north of downtown Los Angeles.
Elevation change: The paved road begins at 2,080′, turns to dirt at 3,480′, and

then climbs to a high point at Inspiration Point of 4,500'. The route drops to 4,400' at Panorama Point before returning to 4,500' and descending on the Sam Merrill Trail to Echo Mountain at 3,207'. This is followed by a climb to 3,480' along Echo Mountain Trail, and then a quick downhill on pavement to 2,080'. Total elevation gain: 2,793'.

Season: This circuit is suited to year-round travel. Winter rains and hot temperatures in the summer are limiting factors. Sweet-smelling Spanish broom is in bloom throughout the spring.

Services: There is a water spigot just past the start of the ride and one at the intersection of Sam Merrill and Echo Mountain Trails. But these sources cannot be guaranteed, so bring all of the water that you will require with you. All services are available in Altadena and neighboring communities of the Los Angeles area.

Hazards: You are likely to see other mountain bikers and hikers using these roads and trails; control your speed while descending. Sam Merrill and Echo Mountain Trails are narrow and contain many obstacles. Walk your bike where necessary. You may encounter Forest Service and utility company vehicles on FS 2N50.

Rescue index: Help can be found in Altadena.

Land status: National forest.

Maps: USGS 7.5 minute quadrangle maps: Mount Wilson and Pasadena.

Finding the trail: From Interstate 210 (east of Los Angeles) take the exit for Lincoln Avenue and follow Lincoln Avenue north through Altadena. After 1.8 miles on Lincoln Avenue, turn right (east) on Loma Alta Drive. Follow Loma Alta Drive for .6 miles to Chaney Trail. Turn left (north) on Chaney Trail. Stay left on Chaney Trail at the "Y" intersection with Alzada Drive. Climb on Chaney Trail approximately 1 mile beyond Alzada Drive to another intersection at a sign for Brown Mountain Road and Millard Canyon. Stay to the right at this intersection and park in the pullout on the right near the locked gate. Do not block the gate.

Sources of additional information:

Angeles National Forest
Arroyo Seco Ranger District
Oak Grove Park
La Canada, CA 91011
(818) 790-1151

Notes on the trail: Pass around the side of the gate and climb on the paved, unsigned FS 2N50. Go past Echo Mountain Trail on the right and continue on FS 2N50 as it turns to dirt. Pass the Mount Lowe Campground on the left after approximately 5 miles of riding on FS 2N50. One-quarter mile beyond the Mount Lowe Campground, turn right at the sign for Inspiration Point. Notice the small sign for Sam Merrill Trail partially hidden by vegetation on the far right. The ride follows Sam Merrill Trail on the return. Continue to Inspiration Point (one-quarter mile from the turnoff of FS 2N50) and on to Panorama Viewpoint at a water tank (1 mile past Inspiration Point). Return the way you came from Panorama Viewpoint and turn left down Sam Merrill Trail (Trail 12W14). Sam Merrill Trail is rough and fragile; to avoid it you can turn left at this point onto FS 2N50 and retrace your path to your car. Taking Sam Merrill Trail will bring you to Echo Mountain Trail. Turn left onto Echo Mountain Trail and pass a water spigot and a trail to Castle Canyon on your left. Continue straight on Echo Mountain Trail to the trail's end at the concrete foundations of White City. Turn around and return on Echo Mountain Trail. Continue on the main trail as side trails branch off. Turn left onto FS 2N50 and descend to your vehicle.

RIDE 23 *RED BOX RINCON ROAD / SHORTCUT CANYON*

This loop covers 23.5 miles. It requires much strength and endurance, as well as good bike handling skills. You will lose elevation for the first 5.6 miles to the West Fork Campground (there is one short, hard uphill). From the campground, ride for 3.2 miles over moderately difficult to strenuous terrain. This is followed by a fast drop on Shortcut Fire Road to the West Fork of the San Gabriel River (there is one brief, steep ascent). The 6.3-mile climb from the river up Shortcut Canyon to the Angeles Crest Highway is unrelenting. The cycling along the highway is one-half "fun descent" and one-half "this would be easy climbing if I weren't so tired."

The first 9.3 miles are on a dirt, four-wheel-drive road in good condition (there is one short, paved section). Shortcut Fire Road is rocky, loose, and sandy. Walking your bike over scree slides may be necessary. The Angeles Crest Highway is a paved, two-lane highway.

Experienced cyclists will enjoy the challenging nature of this excursion. About 12 miles into the trip you come to the West Fork. The river is a welcome sight. Sycamores provide shade and a perfect spot to refresh yourself before beginning the long grind up Shortcut Canyon.

General location: Begins at the Red Box Station parking lot, 14 miles northeast of La Canada Flintridge on the Angeles Crest Highway (CA 2).
Elevation change: The ride commences at Red Box Station at 4,666' and then drops to 3,100' at the West Fork Campground. From here, you ascend to 4,040' at a water tank (near a trail that leads to Newcomb Saddle). From this crest you descend to the West Fork of the San Gabriel River at 3,200' and then pedal up to the Angeles Crest Highway at 4,800'. On the highway you drop to 4,400', climb to 4,800', and end at 4,666'. Add 300' for additional hills encountered en route. Total elevation gain: 3,240'.
Season: Spring and late fall. The uphill on Shortcut Fire Road is too exposed to recommend this loop as a summer ride.

RIDE 23 *RED BOX RINCON ROAD / SHORTCUT CANYON*

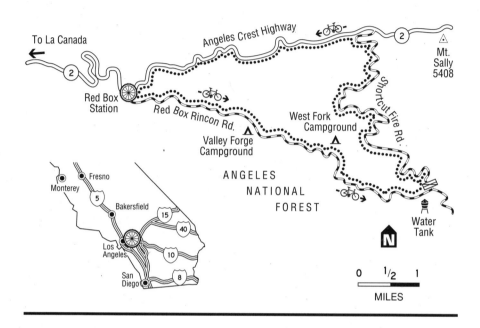

Services: Water, a telephone, and pit toilets are available outside the closed ranger station at Red Box Station. All services can be found in La Canada Flintridge.

Hazards: Vehicular traffic may be encountered on the dirt fire roads described in this ride. Just after the Valley Forge Campground you will negotiate a creek crossing (3.4 miles from the start). It is paved and can be very slick. The descent on Shortcut Fire Road is rocky and steep; lower your saddle and stay in control. The Angeles Crest Highway has little or no shoulder and traffic rushes along. The left turn from the highway into Red Box Station at the end of the loop is particularly dangerous. It is on a blind corner; cyclists may wish to pull over onto the right shoulder, dismount, and walk their bikes across.

Rescue index: Help can be obtained in La Canada Flintridge.

Land status: National forest.

Maps: USGS 7.5 minute quadrangle maps: Chilao Flat and Mount Wilson.

Finding the trail: From Interstate 210 (east of Los Angeles) take the exit for the Angeles Crest Highway (CA 2) in La Canada Flintridge. Drive northeast on the Angeles Crest Highway for approximately 14 miles to the Red Box Station parking lot on the right (south) side of the highway. Park in the parking lot.

Sources of additional information:

Angeles National Forest
701 North Santa Anita Avenue
Arcadia, CA 91006
(818) 574-1613

Notes on the trail: From the parking lot, turn left onto Red Box Rincon Road. After 1 mile of riding you will come to an intersection with signs pointing left toward the Valley Forge and West Fork Campgrounds. Turn left, stay on the main road, and continue past both campgrounds. Three miles beyond the West Fork Campground the road levels out and you pass a water tank and a trail to Newcomb Saddle on the right; continue straight on the main road. Pass the Tumbler Shooting Area on the left. Watch for the signed Shortcut Fire Road on the left as you begin to descend. Turn left (one-half mile beyond the water tank) and pass your bike over the gate to follow Shortcut Fire Road downhill. Ride on Shortcut Fire Road for 9 miles to the Angeles Crest Highway. Turn left and follow the highway to your vehicle.

RIDE 24 *WEST FORK ROAD*

This out-and-back, 13-mile round-trip requires almost no technical skill and a minimum amount of strength. It is about as level a ride as you will find and follows a paved, one-lane road. The road is closed to private motor vehicles.

Cycling on West Fork Road is a pleasant way to spend some time in the San Gabriel Canyon Recreation Area. Do not be discouraged by the graffiti and litter at the start of the ride; it is not a problem after the first quarter mile. After one mile you cross a bridge over Bear Creek, the gorge narrows, and the surrounding vegetation becomes lush. Wildflowers cling to the canyon walls and songbirds are abundant. Small waterfalls line your route during wet periods and inviting pools are found in the creek. The turnaround point is at the Glenn Trail Camp; here you will find six streamside sites with fire rings, picnic tables, pit toilets, and trash cans. The return ride is a fast and enjoyable cruise (you really did climb over 400 feet).

General location: Begins at the intersection of CA 39 and West Fork Road in the San Gabriel Canyon Recreation Area, 11 miles north of Azusa. Azusa is about 20 miles east of downtown Los Angeles.
Elevation change: The ride starts at 1,575' and climbs gradually for 6.5 miles to 2,000'. Total elevation gain: 425'.
Season: Early spring through late fall. Many consider the spring to be the best

RIDE 24   *WEST FORK ROAD*

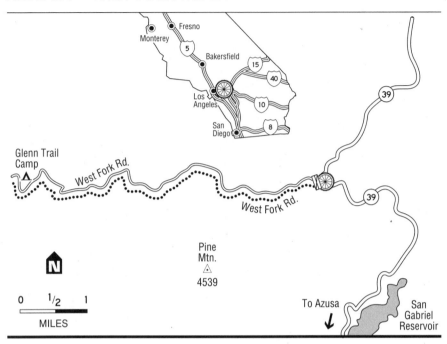

season for biking in the San Gabriel Mountains. Profuse wildflowers, flowing water, and diminished crowds make this a pleasant time for a visit.

Services: There is no water on this ride. All services can be obtained in Azusa.

Hazards: Your main safety concern will be looking out for other trail users. The first 2 miles of this road see heavy use in the summer and on holiday weekends.

Rescue index: Help can be found in Azusa.

Land status: National forest.

Maps: A general map of the Angeles Forest may be obtained at ranger stations throughout the forest; it is a good guide to this ride.

Finding the trail: The trail begins at West Fork Road and San Gabriel Canyon Road (CA 39), 11 miles north of Azusa. From Los Angeles, drive east on Interstate 10 to the exit for Azusa Avenue/CA 39. Follow Azusa Avenue/CA 39 north through the town of Azusa. Entering the San Gabriel Canyon Recreation Area, the road name changes to San Gabriel Canyon Road/CA 39. Keep an eye on the mileposts. West Fork Road begins near milepost 27. There is a parking area on the left near the trailhead. There's more parking and a rest room just a little farther north, across the bridge. On weekends and holidays a parking permit must be purchased to park anywhere in the San Gabriel Canyon Recreation Area.

West Fork Road.

Sources of additional information:

Angeles National Forest
Mount Baldy Ranger District
110 North Wabash Avenue
Glendora, CA 91740
(818) 335-1251

Notes on the trail: Ride west on West Fork Road to the turnaround point at the Glenn Trail Camp. Return the way you came.

RIDE 25 *WEST FORK ROAD / RED BOX RINCON ROAD*

This 30.3-mile loop requires a moderate amount of technical skill. You must be a strong cyclist to manage the ride's length and nearly 4,000 feet of climbing. The first 6.8 miles wind gradually up a paved road to the Glenn Trail Camp. The road rises sharply and continues past the Glenn Trail Camp for three-quarters of a mile to the end of the pavement. The climbing becomes moderately difficult as you move onto dirt. The ascent continues for 6.4 miles and contains occasional steep sections. Then the road rolls up and down steeply as it follows a ridge. After a few more miles, the descents become longer and begin to outnumber the climbs. The trip ends with a welcome 8.4-mile downhill to the highway. Over 70 percent of this ride follows unpaved, four-wheel-drive roads in fair to good condition. Some of the steeper ascents and descents are rocky and worn.

This is an excellent "long" ride with an easy warm-up, moderate climbing, great views, and a rewarding drop at the end.

General location: Begins at the intersection of CA 39 and West Fork Road in the San Gabriel Canyon Recreation Area, 11 miles north of Azusa. Azusa is about 20 miles east of downtown Los Angeles.

Elevation change: The ride starts at 1,575' and climbs to 2,000' at the Glenn Trail Camp. From here the road goes up quickly to 2,270' at Cogswell Dam. A more gradual ascent over the next 5.5 miles brings you to 3,960'. Then the road rises and falls many times for an additional elevation gain of 400' before reaching a high point of 4,840'. From this lofty position the route rolls along for another 200' of climbing. The loop ends with a plummet from 3,600' to 1,600'. Total elevation gain: 3,865'.

Season: Early spring through late fall. There are times when it is sunny in the canyons and cloudy on the mountain ridges; be prepared with an extra layer of warm clothing.

Services: There is no water on this ride. All services are available in Azusa.

Hazards: The first 2 miles of this route can be busy with hikers and fishermen in the summer and on holiday weekends. There may be Forest Service vehicles on the fire roads. Padded cycling gloves are a must for the rapid, bumpy descent to CA 39.

Rescue index: Help can be found in Azusa.

Land status: National forest.

Maps: USGS 7.5 minute quadrangle maps: Azusa, Glendora, and Mount Wilson.

Finding the trail: The trail begins at West Fork Road and San Gabriel Canyon Road (CA 39), 11 miles north of Azusa. From Los Angeles, drive east on Interstate 10 to the exit for Azusa Avenue/CA 39. Follow Azusa Avenue/CA 39 north

RIDE 25 *WEST FORK ROAD / RED BOX RINCON ROAD*

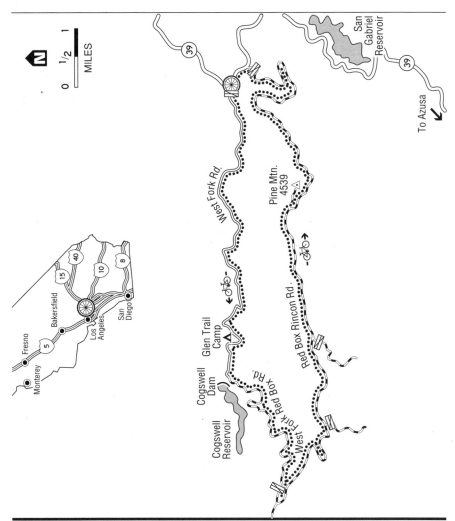

through the town of Azusa. Entering the San Gabriel Canyon Recreation Area, the road name changes to San Gabriel Canyon Road/CA 39. Keep an eye on the mileposts. West Fork Road begins near milepost 27. There's a parking area on the left near the trailhead. There is more parking and a restroom just a little farther north, across the bridge. A permit must be purchased to park anywhere in the San Gabriel Canyon Recreation Area on weekends and holidays.

San Gabriel Canyon Recreation Area from Red Box Rincon Road.

Sources of additional information:

Angeles National Forest
Mount Baldy Ranger District
110 North Wabash Avenue
Glendora, CA 91740
(818) 335-1251

Notes on the trail: Due to the number of unsigned roads found on this loop, a bicycle odometer is recommended for this ride. All mileage notes in the description below are cumulative. Cyclists proficient at route finding may decide that the suggested topographic maps and a compass are sufficient directional aids.

Follow West Fork Road as it climbs past the residences at Cogswell Dam. The road becomes the dirt, West Fork-Red Box Road at mile 7.6. Turn left at the gate at 13.2 miles onto Red Box Rincon Road. You will follow Red Box Rincon Road for more than 16 miles to CA 39. Stay left (uphill) at the intersection at 15.7 miles. Turn left at the intersection at 16.3 miles. Continue straight at 16.7 miles. Turn left at 18.8 miles. At 21.5 miles, stay right and downhill. At 29.9 miles you will arrive at CA 39; turn left and return to your vehicle.

RIDE 26 *MOUNT BALDY*

This is an out-and-back, 9.6-mile round-trip ride up and down Mount Baldy. The first 3.6 miles are a moderately steep ascent of 1,600 feet to the Baldy Notch. A steeper climb of 685 feet in 1.2 miles takes you close to the top of Thunder Mountain. The first one-half mile is on a one-lane paved (but degraded) road. This changes to a hard-packed four-wheel-drive road in good condition with some sections of loose rock. The ride requires a moderate amount of technical riding skill and a good amount of strength.

The roar of rushing water can be heard soon after starting the ride. At the end of the pavement, San Antonio Falls comes into view. A side trail brings you to the base of the 100-foot falls. The dirt road continues to climb up the mountain to the Mount Baldy Ski Lifts Lodge and Baldy Notch. Continuing past the lodge, you arrive at a scree slope that leads to the top of Thunder Mountain. A short hike to the summit affords a terrific view of the surrounding area.

General location: Begins near the end of Mount Baldy Road, approximately 14 miles north of Upland.

Elevation change: The trip gets under way at 6,200', climbs to 7,800' at Baldy Notch, and continues on to 8,485' near the summit of Thunder Mountain. You gain another 100' hiking to the top of Thunder Mountain. Total elevation gain: 2,285' (hike not included).

Season: Late spring through fall. The climb will warm you up, but once at the top you may cool off quickly. Be prepared with extra clothing, especially a windbreaker. Weekends and holidays can be busy.

Services: Water and restrooms are available seasonally at several picnic areas en route to the ride. All services can be found in the town of Mount Baldy, 5 miles south of the trailhead on Mount Baldy Road. The Mount Baldy Ski Lifts Lodge at Baldy Notch includes a cafeteria-style restaurant. It is open on summer weekends.

Hazards: The paved section to San Antonio Falls sees a fair amount of foot traffic; slow down and warn unsuspecting hikers of your approach. Vehicular traffic is restricted but the road is used by the Forest Service and Mount Baldy maintenance workers.

Rescue index: Help is available in the town of Mount Baldy.

Land status: National forest.

Maps: USGS 7.5 minute quadrangle maps: Mount San Antonio and Telegraph Peak.

Finding the trail: Follow Interstate 10 east from Los Angeles and take the exit for Mountain Avenue/Mount Baldy. Stay on Mountain Avenue for 6 miles to reach Mount Baldy Road. Turn right onto Mount Baldy Road and drive north

RIDE 26   *MOUNT BALDY*

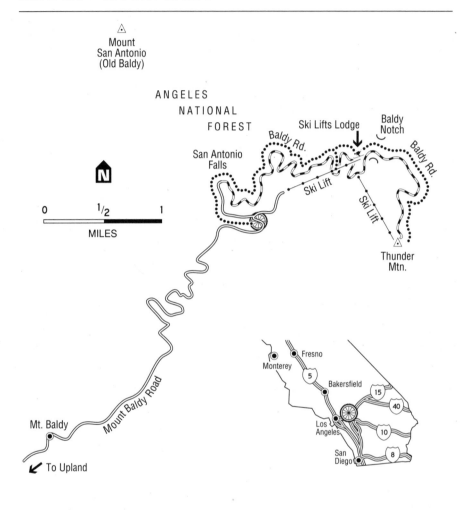

for about 8 miles to the closed Movie Slope Restaurant on the right. The trail begins approximately .3 miles north of the Movie Slope Restaurant; look for a dirt road on the left (west) side of Mount Baldy Road. Park at the start of the dirt road or on the side of Mount Baldy Road.

Sources of additional information:

Angeles National Forest
Mount Baldy Ranger District

110 North Wabash Avenue
Glendora, CA 91740
(818) 335-1251

Notes on the trail: Walk your bike around the gate and follow the road for 3.5 miles to the Mount Baldy Ski Lifts Lodge. Pass the back of the lodge and turn right to follow the road uphill to Baldy Notch and views of the Mojave desert. Stay to the right and climb on the road to its end near the base of Thunder Mountain. Park your bicycle and hike up the scree slope to reach the top of Thunder Mountain. Return the way you came.

RIDE 27 *MORO CANYON*

This is a moderately difficult 9.3-mile loop. Most of the climbing is gradual to moderately steep; there are some demanding uphills on West Loop Trail. Staying in control on the route's steeper downhills will require good bike handling skills. You will encounter some rough terrain descending on Red-Tail Ridge, Rattlesnake, and West Cut-Across trails; expect ruts, washboarding, and loose rocks. The ride follows hard-packed dirt fire roads and single-track trails in mostly good condition.

Although the Crystal Coves backcountry area is shared with equestrians and hikers (no motorized vehicles), it has the reputation of being a "mountain bike park." Cyclists of all abilities will find agreeable trails to explore here. Moro Canyon Trail wanders through oak woodlands and is a pleasant path for beginners. The park's ridge trails, although steep in places, provide dramatic ocean views, challenging single-track riding, and great downhills. In the winter, coastal bluffs provide good vantage points for watching migrating gray whales.

General location: Begins at the Moro Canyon parking lot in Crystal Cove State Park, 2.5 miles north of Laguna Beach and approximately 40 miles south of Los Angeles.
Elevation change: The loop starts at 110' above sea level, drops to 40', and then gradually ascends Moro Canyon to 520'. West Loop Trail quickly climbs to 700' and then follows a ridge line up to Fenceline Trail at 920'. Fenceline Trail rolls up and down and meets Red-Tail Ridge Trail at 920'. It is mostly downhill and rolling terrain from here. End with a 70' ascent back to the trailhead. Tack on another 200' of climbing for undulations encountered over the course of the ride. Total elevation gain: 1,150'.
Season: Crystal Cove State Park is open year-round. Spring visits are pleasant; temperatures are mild and wildflowers are in bloom.
Services: Water, restrooms, and a telephone can be found at the Crystal Cove

RIDE 27 *MORO CANYON*

State Park Ranger Station/Visitor Center. This facility is adjacent to the parking lot. All services are available in the community of Laguna Beach.

Hazards: Descend with care. Sections of Rattlesnake and West Cut-Across Trails are very steep and contain loose rocks and sand. Keep a keen eye out for other trail users; the park gets especially busy on weekends and holidays. Check your clothing and skin periodically for ticks after contact with brush and soil. Poison oak grows near the trail. Rattlesnakes reside in the park.

The grassy hills of Moro Canyon.

Rescue index: Help can be found at the Crystal Cove State Park Ranger Station/ Visitor Center.

Land status: State park.

Maps: A good topographic map of Crystal Cove State Park may be purchased at the Crystal Cove Visitor Center. A local cartographer has produced a mountain bike map of the park utilizing an aerial photograph. This map is also for sale at the Visitor Center.

Finding the trail: The ride begins from the Moro Canyon parking lot in Crystal Cove State Park. The park fronts the Pacific Coast Highway (CA 1), approximately 2.5 miles north of Laguna Beach and approximately 2 miles south of Newport Beach. From the highway, look for a small sign marking the entrance to Moro Canyon. Turn east into the park entrance and proceed to the entrance station. A day-use fee is required for parking.

Sources of additional information:

California Department of Parks and Recreation
Orange Coast District
18331 Enterprise Lane
Huntington Beach, CA 92648
(714) 848-1566

Crystal Cove Interpretive Association
P.O. Box 4352
Laguna Beach, CA 92652
(714) 494-3539

Notes on the trail: Start the ride near the entrance station in the southeast corner of the parking area; you will find a trail here marked by an "Official Vehicles Only" sign. Follow this trail past a trailer park and down to the signed Moro Canyon Trail. Go uphill on Moro Canyon Trail. You will arrive at a hub of trails after 3 miles of pedaling. Turn left here onto West Loop Trail where Moro Canyon Trail continues right. Climb for approximately 1.3 miles on West Loop Trail to a gate at single-track Fenceline Trail. Turn left onto Fenceline Trail and follow it for .5 miles to a "T" intersection. Turn left at this intersection onto Red-Tail Ridge Trail. After .8 miles, Red-Tail Ridge Trail narrows and becomes the single-track Rattlesnake Trail. Continue for 1 mile on Rattlesnake Trail to an electrical tower. Follow Rattlesnake Trail as it turns hard to the right here and widens to become a fire road. Follow the fire road for .8 miles to an intersection at West Cut-Across Trail. Turn left and follow West Cut-Across Trail down to Moro Canyon Trail. Turn right onto Moro Canyon Trail and return the way you came.

A portion of Crystal Cove State Park is designated as an underwater park. Scuba divers and snorkelers can explore reefs and kelp beds in a unique marine environment. There are 3.5 miles of beach and marine preserve with 32 walk-in environmental campsites. Contact the park for details.

RIDE 28 *BELL CANYON*

Bell Canyon loop is a 5.6-mile circuit in the Ronald W. Caspers Wilderness Park. The riding on Bell Canyon Trail is easy, with some short hills. Sun Rise and East Ridge Trails require additional effort, for they are steep in places. The route follows dirt fire roads in fair condition. At the time of our research, Sun Rise and East Ridge Trails had been graded recently and were rock strewn and soft. We expect the road surfaces to improve with time and traffic.

This large wilderness park, located in the western Santa Ana Mountains, has

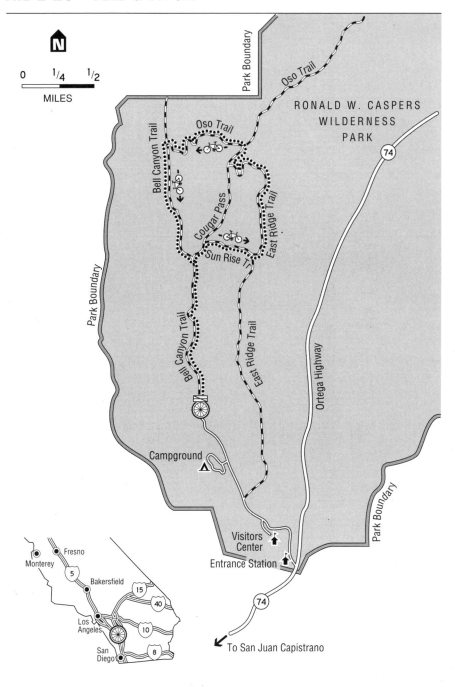

Ronald W. Caspers Wilderness Park.

over 15 miles of dirt roads suitable for mountain biking. Beginners can follow the scenic Bell Canyon Trail as it rambles past woodlands, grasslands, and streams. Advanced cyclists can explore the park's more challenging terrain.

General location: Begins at the Old Corral Picnic Area in Ronald W. Caspers Wilderness Park, 7.5 miles east of the city of San Juan Capistrano, and approximately 60 miles southeast of downtown Los Angeles.

Elevation change: The trip starts at 470' on Bell Canyon Trail and ascends gradually to 530' at the intersection with Sun Rise Trail. The route then rises rapidly to 800' at the intersection with East Ridge Trail. Following East Ridge Trail, you drop to 760', and then climb moderately to 900' at Pointed Hill. This is followed by a quick descent to the intersection with Cougar Pass Trail at 700', and then rolling terrain to 720' at the intersection with Oso Trail. On Oso Trail you descend for .5 miles to Bell Canyon at 570'. From here it is a cruise down the canyon to the trailhead at 470'. Total elevation gain: 490'.

Season: Cyclists can enjoy this park at any time of the year. Trail use is light in the early spring, late fall, and winter.

Services: Water and restrooms are available at the Old Corral Picnic Area. All services can be obtained in San Juan Capistrano.

Hazards: The rangers at the entrance station do a good job of informing you that you are entering a wilderness area characterized by certain dangers. Besides rattlesnakes, poison oak, and rugged terrain, they stress that mountain lions live within the park, that they are unpredictable and dangerous. Minors have been attacked and are restricted to the Visitor Center and picnic areas. They must be accompanied by an adult. Riding alone is prohibited. This park is popular with equestrians. Stay alert, especially when approaching blind corners. Loose rocks and sand make the steep descents on East Ridge and Oso Trails treacherous.

Rescue index: Help can be found at the entrance station during daylight hours. There is a pay phone at the Visitor Center. You must purchase a wilderness permit when you enter the park. Carry it with you while riding or hiking.

Land status: County park.

Maps: A Caspers Wilderness Trail Guide is available at the park entrance station and is a good guide to this trail.

Finding the trail: Follow Interstate 5 to San Juan Capistrano and take the exit for Ortega Highway (CA 74). Travel east on CA 74 for 7.5 miles to the entrance of Ronald W. Caspers Wilderness Park on the left. Pay a day-use fee at the entrance station and proceed to the extreme north end of the park's main road. Park your vehicle in the dirt parking area at the Old Corral Picnic Area.

Sources of additional information:

Ronald W. Caspers Wilderness Park
33401 Ortega Highway
P.O. Box 395
San Juan Capistrano, CA 92675-0395
(714) 728-0235 or 831-2174

Notes on the trail: All of the trails in this park are well marked, and the intersections are numbered. Begin this ride on Bell Canyon Trail, the dirt road that begins at a locked gate at the north end of the parking area. After 1 mile, turn right toward East Ridge Trail at signpost #14. Soon after, continue straight onto Sun Rise Trail at signpost #16 where Cougar Pass Trail goes left. Ride uphill to signpost #17. Stay to the left here to follow East Ridge Trail north. Keep to the left at signpost #19 near Pointed Hill. Descend to Cougar Pass Trail and stay to the right at signpost #18. Climb to Oso Trail at signpost #21 and turn left. Cycle to Bell Canyon Trail at signpost #20 and turn left. Follow Bell Canyon Trail downhill to the trailhead.

You may wish to walk the Caspers Nature Trail after your ride. It is located south of the Bell Canyon Trailhead near the old corral and windmill. The Visitor Center contains photographic displays and interpretive exhibits of the park's history and natural features.

Bicycles are restricted to the park's dirt roads. Stay off the horse and hiking trails.

RIDE 29 *DELAMAR MOUNTAIN*

This 10.5-mile loop requires a moderate amount of strength. The ascent, though only steep for the first one-half mile, is steady and 4.5 miles long. The downhill is fast and potholed, requiring good riding technique. Most of the trip is on unpaved, two-wheel-drive roads in good condition. The first one-half mile and the last two miles are on pavement.

This route is an excellent introduction to mountain biking in the Big Bear Lake region. It is quite easy and takes in some great scenery. As the road winds up and around Delamar Mountain, views open up to include Big Bear Lake, the San Gorgonio Wilderness, and the San Gabriel Mountains. The roads receive good sun exposure and are often free of snow in the early spring.

General location: Begins in the town of Fawnskin, approximately 60 miles east of Los Angeles.

Elevation change: Starts at 7,000' and reaches a high point of 7,500' on Forest Service Road 2N71. The route descends on dirt to CA 38 at 6,775' and ends back at 7,000' in Fawnskin. Ups and downs along the way add an estimated 100' of climbing to the ride. Total elevation gain: 825'.

Season: Spring and fall afford the best temperatures for riding. Nights can be cold, so be prepared if you plan to camp. The region becomes busy with vacationers in the summer.

Services: There is no water on this ride. All services are available in Fawnskin and nearby communities.

Hazards: "Street-legal" vehicles are permitted on the fire roads in the forest. Campgrounds are located off these roads and there is bound to be some traffic. If at all possible, avoid weekends and holidays from Memorial Day until Labor Day. Care should be taken on CA 38; this stretch of highway contains some blind corners.

Rescue index: Assistance can be found in the town of Fawnskin or at the Big Bear Ranger Station. The ranger station is located on the north side of Big Bear Lake on CA 38, 3 miles east of Fawnskin.

Land status: National forest.

Maps: USGS 7.5 minute quadrangle map: Fawnskin. You can obtain an information sheet on mountain biking and a general map of the area at the Big Bear Ranger Station.

Finding the trail: From Interstate 10 in Redlands, take the Orange Street off-ramp. Head north on Orange Street for .5 miles and turn right (east) onto Lugonia Avenue (CA 38). Follow CA 38 for approximately 60 miles to Big Bear Lake. Follow the highway across the Stanfield Cutoff (a road over an earthen dam) to the north side of the lake. Turn left (west) to stay on CA 38 towards Fawnskin.

RIDE 29 *DELAMAR MOUNTAIN*

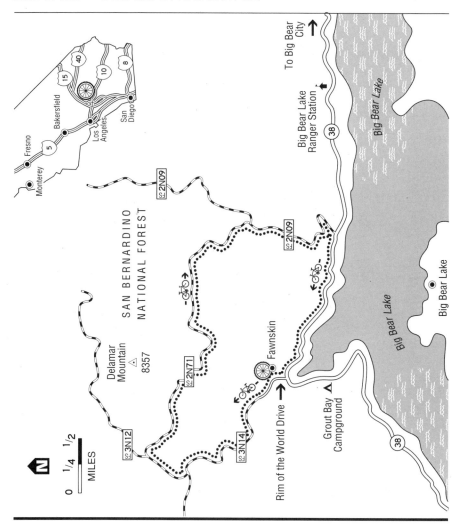

Pass the Big Bear Ranger Station after 1 mile. Three miles beyond the ranger station you will enter the town of Fawnskin. Automobiles may be parked in legal zones on the streets of Fawnskin.

Sources of additional information:

San Bernardino National Forest
Big Bear Ranger District

Big Bear Lake from Delamar Mountain.

P.O. Box 290
Fawnskin, CA 92333
(714) 866-3437

Big Bear Visitor Center
North Shore Drive, Highway 38
(3 miles east of Fawnskin)

Notes on the trail: In Fawnskin, follow Rim of the World Drive north. Soon the pavement ends and the road becomes FS 3N14. After approximately 2 miles of riding you will intersect with FS 3N12. Turn right onto FS 3N12. Ride about .5 miles to an intersection with FS 2N71 and turn right. Stay on FS 2N71 as it traverses the south side of Delamar Mountain. Turn right at the intersection with FS 2N09. Follow FS 2N09 downhill to CA 38. Turn right onto CA 38 and follow the highway for 2 miles back to Fawnskin.

RIDE 30 *ARCTIC CANYON OVERLOOK*

Here is a challenging ride for experienced cyclists. This 19.5-mile loop includes demanding climbs and steep, technical descents. Approximately 15 miles of the trip is on unpaved, two-wheel-drive roads in good condition. After five miles of pedaling, the route becomes a bouldered, sometimes sandy four-wheel-drive road. Later it turns into a rough motorcycle trail. There are uphill sections where the trail is rocky, rutted, and soft. This extremely rough portion is five miles long. The last ten miles of the loop are on good dirt roads.

Upon reaching Arctic Canyon Overlook you will catch a glimpse of the desert off to the east. Take some time to scramble up the rocks and take in the marvelous view of Arctic Canyon, the Lucerne Valley, and the East Mojave Desert.

Local cyclists speak of a ghost that haunts the forest and decides who will stay in the saddle and "clean" this ride. May the ghost be with you.

General location: Begins in the town of Big Bear City, approximately 60 miles east of Los Angeles.

Elevation change: The ride starts at 6,830' and climbs for 3.5 miles to 7,390'. From here it levels off for a mile, and then ascends again for nearly 4 miles to a high point of 8,000'. Next the trail drops to 7,500' before rising again, this time to 7,750'. The route continues by going downhill to 7,300', rolling down and up to 7,400', and finally descending back to the start at 6,830'. Rolling topography adds an estimated 200' of climbing to the ride. Total elevation gain: 1,720'.

Season: Late spring through fall. The Big Bear Lake region can get very busy in the summer.

Services: There is no water on this ride. All services are available in Big Bear City.

Hazards: Forest Service Road 3N32 can be treacherous; the utmost care should be taken on the downhill sections of this road. Due to the popularity of Holcomb Valley Campground in the summer, FS 3N16 can become busy with motor vehicles; avoid weekends and holidays between Memorial Day and Labor Day.

Rescue index: Help may be obtained in Big Bear City or at the Big Bear Ranger Station on CA 38.

Land status: National forest.

Maps: USGS 7.5 minute quadrangle maps: Fawnskin and Big Bear City. Carry also the San Bernardino National Forest map.

Finding the trail: From Interstate 10 in Redlands, take the Orange Street exit. Head north on Orange Street for .5 miles and turn right (east) onto Lugonia Avenue (CA 38). Follow CA 38 for approximately 60 miles to Big Bear Lake. Follow the highway across the Stanfield Cutoff (a road over an earthen dam) to the north side of the lake. Turn right (east) onto CA 18 toward Big Bear City. After about 2 miles you will see a sign for Van Dusen Canyon and Holcomb

RIDE 30   *ARCTIC CANYON OVERLOOK*

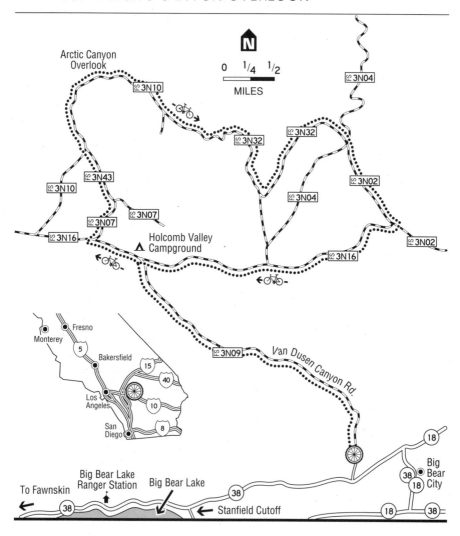

Valley. Turn left (north) here onto Van Dusen Canyon Road and follow it to the end of the pavement. Park in the large dirt pullout on the right.

Sources of additional information:

San Bernardino National Forest
Big Bear Ranger District
P.O. Box 290

The Lucerne Valley from Arctic Canyon Overlook.

Fawnskin, CA 92333
(714) 866-3437

Big Bear Visitor Center
North Shore Drive, Highway 38
(3 miles east of Fawnskin)

Notes on the trail: Many of the Forest Service roads described in this ride are unmarked. We suggest that you use the recommended maps and a compass as directional aids.

Follow the signed FS 3N09 north for 3.6 miles to FS 3N16 at a sign for Holcomb Valley Campground. Turn left onto FS 3N16. Ride for about 1 mile on FS 3N16 to FS 3N07 on the right at a sign for Wilbur's Grave and Arctic Canyon. Turn right and follow FS 3N07 for .5 miles to FS 3N43 on the left. Turn left onto FS 3N43 and follow it for 1.8 miles to the unsigned Arctic Canyon Overlook. Although no signs indicate a change, you are now on FS 3N10. Continue past the overlook for about a mile to an unmarked fork in the road. Stay left. There is an obscure landmark just after you stay left at the fork—a sign on the left that reads "Greenhorn Claim." It is partially hidden by trees. It is 1.1 miles from this landmark to a "T" intersection at FS 3N32. Turn right onto FS 3N32. A short distance down the road brings you to another poorly marked intersection. A sign reads "No Green Sticker Vehicles." Turn left here to continue on FS 3N32. From this turn it is 1.5 miles to FS 3N02. Turn right onto FS 3N02 and follow it for 1.3 miles to FS 3N16. Turn right onto FS 3N16. Follow this road for approximately 3 miles to FS 3N09 on the left. Turn left onto FS 3N09 and descend back to your vehicle.

RIDE 31 *SKYLINE DRIVE*

Here is a hard, 18.3-mile loop that is well worth the effort involved. You begin with a three-mile climb that is steep for the first mile and then becomes less difficult. Once "The Skyline" is reached the riding becomes easier. As you cycle along the ridge you traverse a series of hills; you are losing elevation overall. After passing the trail to Grandview Point, there are several short climbs and two moderately steep ascents that are both over a mile long. There is plenty of descending. Two-thirds of the ride is on two-wheel-drive dirt roads. These are in good condition with some washboarding on some of the steeper sections. There is one mile of good single-track trail. The remainder of the trip is on paved roads in good condition.

An abundance of top-notch fire roads have helped make the Big Bear Lake area a mecca for mountain bikers. Skyline Drive is a favorite of locals and visitors alike. In addition to a great road surface, it offers spectacular scenery. Grandview Point is the best place to take in the view of 11,510-foot San Gorgonio Mountain and Ten Thousand Foot Ridge.

General location: Begins at the Snow Summit Ski Area, in the town of Big Bear Lake, approximately 60 miles east of Los Angeles.
Elevation change: The ride starts at 7,040' and climbs to a high point of 8,100'. The trail undulates after reaching the ridge, adding an estimated 1,000' of climbing to the ride. Total elevation gain: 2,060'.
Season: Late spring through fall. Mornings and evenings can be brisk, but day-

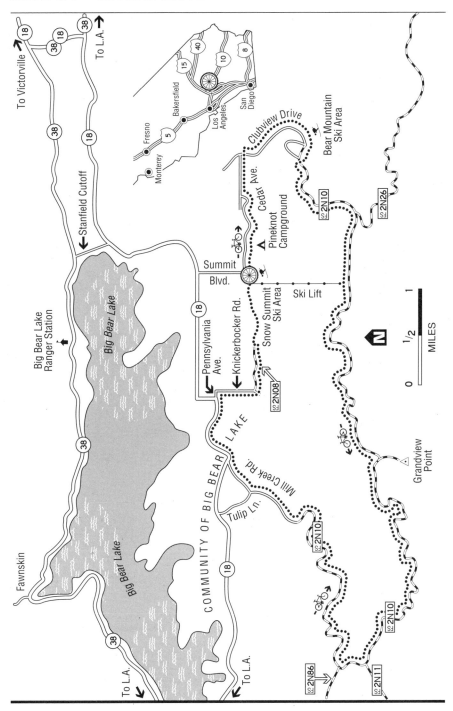

View from the Skyline.

time temperatures are perfect for riding. Avoid the crowds by planning to visit Big Bear Lake before Memorial Day or after Labor Day.

Services: There is no water on this ride. All services are available in the town of Big Bear Lake.

Hazards: Ride defensively and predictably, especially near the end of the loop where you will be traveling through Big Bear Lake on CA 18. Watch for traffic at all times. The last mile of the trip is on a twisty, downhill single-track trail.

Rescue index: Help can be found in the town of Big Bear Lake.
Land status: National forest.
Maps: USGS 7.5 minute quadrangle maps: Big Bear Lake and Moonridge.
Finding the trail: From Interstate 10 in Redlands, take the Orange Street exit. Follow Orange Street north for .5 miles and turn right (east) onto Lugonia Avenue (CA 38). Follow CA 38 for approximately 60 miles to Big Bear Lake and CA 18. Follow CA 18 around the south side of the lake to reach the community of Big Bear Lake. Go left (south) on Summit Boulevard for about 1 mile to the Snow Summit Ski Area parking lot.

Sources of additional information:

San Bernardino National Forest
Big Bear Ranger District
P.O. Box 290
Fawnskin, CA 92333
(714) 866-3437

Team Big Bear Mountain Bike Center
P.O. Box 3765
880 Summit Boulevard
Big Bear Lake, CA 92315
(714) 866-4565

Notes on the trail: The ride begins in the southeast corner of the Snow Summit Ski Area parking lot. Follow the sign toward the Pine Knot Campground on paved Cedar Avenue. Ride past the campground. The road changes to dirt and turns to the left before coming to the "T" intersection of Cedar Avenue and Switzerland Drive. Turn right to continue on Cedar Avenue. After .5 miles you will reach another "T" intersection at Clubview Drive. Turn right and climb on Clubview Drive past the Bear Mountain Ski Area. A short distance beyond the ski area the road changes to a dirt surface. Soon after leaving the pavement you arrive at the signed Forest Service Road 2N10. Turn left onto FS 2N10. You will stay on FS 2N10 for nearly 13 miles. Fourteen miles from the start of the ride you enter a residential area where the road surface turns to pavement. The road name changes at this point from FS 2N10 to Mill Creek Road. After 1.3 miles on pavement you arrive at the intersection of Mill Creek Road and Tulip Lane. Turn right to stay on Mill Creek Road. Continue on Mill Creek Road for another .5 miles to Big Bear Boulevard (CA 18). Turn right onto Big Bear Boulevard (CA 18). Follow it through town for .8 miles to Pine Knot Drive. Continue straight onto Pennsylvania Avenue where CA 18 goes left and follows Pine Knot Drive. After .2 miles on Pennsylvania Avenue, turn right onto Knickerbocker Road. Climb on this paved road for .5 miles where you will see FS 2N08, a dirt road, to your left. Turn left onto FS 2N08 and follow it a short distance to where the road becomes a single-track trail. Go around some boulders that partially block the trail. Stay on this single-track for 1 mile, passing behind residential developments to the parking lot of the Snow Summit Ski Area and your parked vehicle.

"The Skyline" is also accessible to less energetic cyclists. For a fee, you and your bike can ride a Snow Summit chair lift to the ridge. Make inquiries at the Team Big Bear Mountain Bike Center at the Snow Summit Ski Area.

RIDE 32 *DUNN ROAD*

This 17-mile, mostly downhill one-way ride involves a shuttle to the trailhead. Portions of the descent are steep, rocky, and require a fair amount of technical skill. Most of the biking is on an unpaved, two-wheel-drive road in good condition, but there is some washboarding. The first 6.5 miles climb gradually and include some short, very steep stretches.

Dunn Road takes you from the high desert of the Santa Rosa Mountains to the low desert of the Coachella Valley. Numerous cacti and wildflowers are in bloom in March and April. Outstanding views include the rugged San Jacinto Mountains to the west and the Coachella Valley backed by the Little San Bernardino Mountains to the northeast. The most alluring quality of this ride is that it is mostly downhill; you lose over 3,000 feet of elevation!

General location: Begins off CA 74, 16.5 miles southwest of Palm Desert, near the Atajo Alpine Village subdivision.

Elevation change: The ride starts at 4,265' and ends at 1,150'. There is approximately 500' of climbing and 3,315' of elevation loss. Not bad, eh?

Season: Late fall through early spring. Summer riding is not recommended; it can get very hot. Take plenty of water.

Services: There is no water on this ride. All services are available in the communities along CA 111 in the Coachella Valley.

Hazards: Automobiles and off-road vehicles use this road. Control your speed on the rocky and washboarded portions of the descent. Expect sudden weather changes. The temperature at the trailhead will be considerably cooler than in the low desert; take warm clothing with you.

Rescue index: Help can be found at the end of the ride in Cathedral City and possibly in the neighborhood of Atajo Alpine Village at the start of the ride.

Land status: Bureau of Land Management lands.

Maps: USGS 7.5 minute quadrangle maps: Cathedral City, Rancho Mirage, and Toro Peak.

Finding the trail: The described ride involves a two-vehicle shuttle. Drive two cars to the intersection of East Palm Canyon Drive/CA 111 and Cathedral Canyon Drive in Cathedral City. Proceed south on Cathedral Canyon Drive for .5 miles to Terrace Road. Turn right (west) on Terrace Road and follow it for

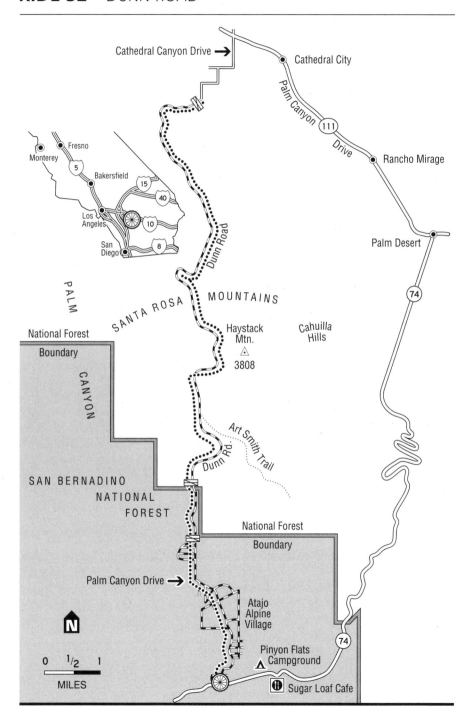

Looking toward Cathedral Canyon from Dunn Road.

.3 miles to Vista Drive. Go left (south) onto Vista Drive and travel .3 miles to Grandview Avenue. Turn right (west) on Grandview Avenue. Grandview Avenue ends after .4 miles where it connects with Elna Way on the left. Turn left (south) at the end of Grandview Avenue onto Elna Way. Stay on Elna Way for .3 miles to Carroll Drive on the right. Turn right (southwest) onto Carroll Drive. Follow Carroll Drive .1 miles to its terminus at Channel Drive. At the end of Carroll Drive, look across Channel Drive to locate a locked gate that blocks a dirt road. The dirt road is the northern extreme of Dunn Road, where you will finish your bike ride. Park one vehicle curbside on Carroll Drive. Return the way you came in the second vehicle to the intersection of East Palm Canyon Drive/CA 111 and Cathedral Canyon Drive. Turn right (east) onto East Palm Canyon Drive/CA 111 and drive 6.3 miles to CA 74 in Palm Desert. Go right (south) onto CA 74. After 15.4 miles on CA 74, you pass the Sugar Loaf Cafe on the left, and then the San Bernardino National Forest Pinyon Flats Campground on the right at 15.8 miles. Just .7 miles further brings you to Palm Canyon Drive on the right (after 16.5 miles on CA 74). Turn right (north) onto Palm Canyon Drive. This dirt road enters a residential development named Atajo Alpine Village. Park on the side of Palm Canyon Drive; do not block the mailboxes.

Sources of additional information:

Bureau of Land Management
P.O. Box 2000

North Palm Springs, CA 92258-2000
(619) 251-0812

Notes on the trail: Begin the ride at the intersection of Palm Canyon Drive and CA 74. Follow Palm Canyon Drive north through Atajo Alpine Village subdivision. Go around a locked gate after 2.8 miles of riding. Travel 1 mile farther and arrive at another locked gate; a sign marks the National Forest Boundary here. Pass your bike over the gate and continue straight (you are now traveling on Dunn Road). About 2 miles beyond the last gate you come to an intersection where a well-beaten cow path veers to the left. Stay to the right, paralleling a fence, and follow the main road uphill. In another mile, continue straight where the Art Smith Trail goes right. A short distance beyond the Art Smith Trail, you pass picnic tables and a chemical toilet at a viewpoint. Stay on the main road and follow it down to the locked gate at Channel and Carroll Drives. Lift your bike over the gate and ride to your parked vehicle.

RIDE 33 THOMAS MOUNTAIN ROAD

Completing this 23-mile loop requires strength and good conditioning. You begin with a long, moderate ascent of 7.7 miles. There are several "breaks" in the climb. The ride down the mountain is steep and fun. You will complete the circuit on six miles of paved, mostly level roads. Thomas Mountain Road is an unpaved, two-wheel-drive road in predominantly good condition. Some rutting and gravel can be expected on the descent.

Cool temperatures and great scenery along a well-graded mountain road make this tour a favorite among local mountain bikers. For an overnight experience, good camping is available at three primitive campgrounds near the mountain summit.

General location: 32 miles southwest of Palm Desert on CA 74.
Elevation change: The trip begins in the Garner Valley at 4,430' and climbs to 6,750' on Thomas Mountain. Total elevation gain: 2,320'
Season: Spring through fall. This is a good summer ride, a nice way to beat the heat of the nearby desert.
Services: There is no water on this ride. Water, food, gas, telephones, and a campground can be found at the Hemet Market (1 mile northwest of the trailhead on CA 74). All services are available in Hemet, approximately 25 miles northwest of Thomas Mountain Road on CA 74.
Hazards: It can get very cold in the spring and fall. Be prepared with dry underlayers to change into after completing the climb. Bring also a jacket and warm gloves. Keep your speed under control on the descent and watch for cars ap-

RIDE 33 *THOMAS MOUNTAIN ROAD*

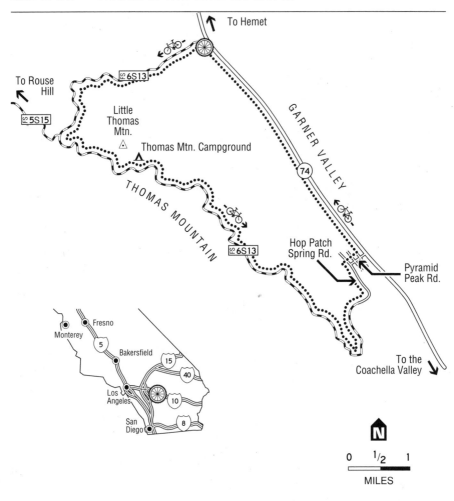

proaching from around blind corners. Some gravel and sand can be expected on the downhill. There is moderately heavy traffic along CA 74 on weekends and holidays.

Rescue index: Help can be found in Hemet, approximately 25 miles northwest of the trailhead, or in the Coachella Valley about 32 miles to the northeast. There are pay phones at Hemet Market 1 mile northwest of the start of the ride.

Land status: National forest.

Thomas Mountain Road.

Maps: The San Bernardino National Forest map is a good guide to the roads followed on this loop.

Finding the trail: The ride begins at the intersection of CA 74 and Thomas Mountain Road (Forest Service Road 6S13), 32 miles southwest of Palm Desert. From points east, and CA 111 in Palm Desert, drive south on CA 74. You will pass a sign for Thomas Mountain Road on the left (west) side of the highway after 27 miles. This is where you will come off Thomas Mountain. Continue another 5 miles on CA 74 to the other end of Thomas Mountain Road on the left (west) side of the highway. From points west, follow CA 74 east. Drive through Hemet and continue on CA 74 for approximately 25 miles to the Hemet Market at Lake Hemet on the right. Go beyond the Hemet Market for 1 mile to Thomas Mountain Road on the right (west) side of CA 74. Turn west onto Thomas Mountain Road and park on the roadside.

Sources of additional information:

San Bernardino National Forest
San Jacinto Ranger District
P.O. Box 518
54270 Pinecrest
Idyllwild, CA 92349
(714) 659-2117

Notes on the trail: Follow Thomas Mountain Road (FS 6S13) west, away from the highway. Continue on Thomas Mountain Road (FS 6S13) where FS 5S15 goes right toward Rouse Hill. After passing the Thomas Mountain Campground you will begin a long descent. Stay on the main road through the forest and pass Ramona Camp and Toolbox Springs Camp. About 6 miles beyond Toolbox Springs Camp, you enter a residential area and the road surface changes to pavement. The road name changes here to Hop Patch Springs Road. Continue on Hop Patch Springs Road for approximately 1 mile to Pyramid Peak Road. Turn right onto Pyramid Peak Road and follow it .4 miles to CA 74. Turn left onto CA 74 and ride about 5 miles to Thomas Mountain Road on the left. Turn left to reach your parked vehicle.

RIDE 34 *LOS PENASQUITOS CANYON*

This is an easy, out-and-back, 12-mile round-trip ride. The terrain is gentle over an unpaved two-wheel-drive road that is in good condition for most of its length. The road does have a few sandy spots, and some of the short hills contain loose rocks and ruts.

Los Penasquitos Canyon is six miles in length and lies in the midst of San Diego suburbia. Just a few minutes of pedaling will take you into the deep shade of sycamores, eucalyptus, live oak, pepper trees, and willows. The name, Los Penasquitos, means "the little cliffs," and alludes to the rocky bluffs that are visible from the road. Adobe structures built by Mexican settlers can be found at both ends of the park. The restored building at the eastern extreme, the Johnson-Taylor Adobe, was once the center of activity in the canyon and now claims the honor of being San Diego's oldest rancho.

General location: Begins at the Los Penasquitos Canyon Preserve, 24 miles north of San Diego.

Elevation change: The ride starts at approximately 250'. You descend to 100' at the west end of the canyon—the turnaround point. Several small hills add an estimated 50' of climbing to the ride. Total elevation gain: 200'.

Season: This trail can be ridden year-round. Wildflowers and light traffic in the early spring make this a good time to visit. Use is heavy on weekends and holidays, and the trail is popular in the late afternoon with people seeking exercise after work.

Services: You will find a water fountain and a chemical toilet at the trailhead. Bring your own water, for the water fountain is an unreliable source. All services are available in San Diego and surrounding communities.

Hazards: This route is used heavily. You are likely to encounter equestrians,

RIDE 34 *LOS PENASQUITOS CANYON*

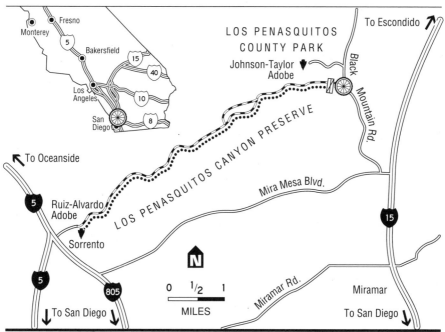

hikers, picnickers, families, and children on school outings. Familiarize yourself with guidelines of responsible trail cycling; be courteous and use common sense. Rattlesnakes inhabit the canyon and play an important role in the park's ecology.

Rescue index: Help can be found in the nearby community of Miramar.

Land status: This area is a preserve of the City and County of San Diego.

Maps: USGS 7.5 minute quadrangle maps: Del Mar and Poway Valley.

Finding the trail: The trail begins at the Los Penasquitos Canyon Preserve, 24 miles north of San Diego. From San Diego, take Interstate 15 to the exit for Mira Mesa Boulevard. Follow Mira Mesa Boulevard west to Black Mountain Road. Go right (north) on Black Mountain Road for 2 miles to the Los Penasquitos Canyon Preserve entrance on the left (west) side of the road. Parking is available for day use only.

Sources of additional information:

County of San Diego Parks and Recreation
5201 Ruffin Road (029)
San Diego, CA 92123
(619) 694-3049

Los Penasquitos Canyon.

San Diego County Archaeology Society
P.O. Box A-81106
San Diego, CA 92138
(619) 694-2828

Notes on the trail: The trailhead is located at the northwest end of the Los Penasquitos Canyon Preserve parking lot. Lift your bike over the gate and follow the road to the turnaround point at the Ruiz-Alvarado Adobe. Return the way you came. Many of the preserve's trails are closed to bicycles; please obey all of the signs indicating closings.

The Johnson-Taylor Adobe House can be reached by entering the Penasquitos Community Park entrance, .3 miles north of the Los Penasquitos Canyon Preserve entrance on Black Mountain Road. Follow the Penasquitos Community Park entrance road west past the playing fields to the adobes.

RIDE 35 *GREEN VALLEY LOOP*

This is a five-mile trip consisting of a four-mile loop and a one-mile out-and-back spur. The riding is easy to moderately difficult with some short, steep sections of trail. The fire roads and trails here are in fair to good condition. Hoof prints,

RIDE 35 GREEN VALLEY LOOP

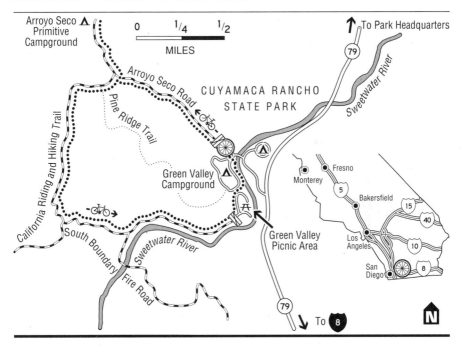

rutting, and loose rocks are found on the portion of the route that follows the California Riding and Hiking Trail.

This ride begins among mature stands of canyon live oak and ponderosa pine. You soon enter a chaparral plant community that allows unobstructed views from the trail into the park's interior valleys. Near the end of the ride you will reach the Sweetwater River and the Green Valley Falls. Several still pools dot the river, their reflective surface broken only by the occasional bather.

General location: Commences at the Green Valley Campground and Picnic Area in Cuyamaca Rancho State Park, approximately 40 miles east of San Diego.
Elevation change: The ride begins at 3,957' and climbs to 4,290' at the Arroyo Seco Primitive Campground. Undulations in the trail add an estimated 200' of climbing to the ride. Total elevation gain: 533'.
Season: Seasonal color and comfortable temperatures make the spring and fall ideal times for riding in Cuyamaca Rancho State Park. This region sees heavy use during the summer months and also on weekends and holidays. Be prepared for cool evening temperatures if you are planning on camping here in the spring or fall.
Services: Water, rest rooms, phone, interpretive information, and camping (in-

Green Valley Trail.

cluding showers) are available at the Green Valley Campground. All services can be found at Lake Cuyamaca, just north of the park on CA 79.

Hazards: Part of this ride is on the California Riding and Hiking Trail. Keep an eye out for equestrians. The route may be hoof worn and rock strewn in places. The park's bicycle speed limit is 15 m.p.h.

Rescue index: Help is available at the Cuyamaca Rancho State Park Headquarters, 2 miles north of the Green Valley Campground and Picnic Area on CA 79.

Land status: State park.

Maps: A map of Cuyamaca Rancho State Park may be purchased at the park headquarters. It is a good guide to this ride.

Finding the trail: Cuyamaca Rancho State Park is located on CA 79, about 10 miles south of Julian. From San Diego, take Interstate 8 east to the exit for CA 79. Follow CA 79 north for approximately 9 miles to the Green Valley Campground and Picnic Area on the left (west) side of the highway. Turn left and follow the campground entrance road as it swings right (north). Stop and pay a day-use parking fee at the fee station on the right. Continue in a northerly direction and go past the first campground. Cross the river and turn right into the second day-use parking area. Park your vehicle.

Sources of additional information:

>Cuyamaca Rancho State Park
>12551 Highway 79
>Descanso, CA 92016
>(619) 765-0755

Notes on the trail: From the day-use parking area, follow the signed Arroyo Seco Road for 1 mile to the sign for Green Valley. Continue straight for .5 miles to the Arroyo Seco Primitive Campground. Turn around and return to the intersection with the sign for Green Valley. Turn right here to follow the California Riding and Hiking Trail. In .3 miles, continue straight on the California Riding and Hiking Trail where Pine Ridge Hiking Trail goes left. Stay left at all the remaining intersections to reach pavement at the Green Valley Picnic Area. Follow the exit signs north through the campground to your vehicle.

RIDE 36 *STONEWALL MINE*

This is a 12.5-mile loop with an out-and-back spur to Stonewall Mine. The difficulty of the ride varies along its course. The first few miles are on an excellent two-wheel-drive dirt road that is suitable for beginning cyclists. The ride continues onto Soapstone Grade Road, which contains steep sections as well as areas of rock and sand. The spur out to Stonewall Mine is in good condition and the riding is quite easy. The descent on Stonewall Creek Fire Road requires good bike handling ability; the trail is sandy and rock strewn in places.

The cycling is cool for the first 3.5 miles as you travel through a shady forest of large California black oaks, live oaks, and ponderosa pines. As the trail climbs further, you ride through chaparral, sage, yucca, and cacti. The descent along Stonewall Creek Fire Road is lined with riparian vegetation—sycamore, alder, cottonwood, and willow.

The historical site of Stonewall Mine has a sealed-off mine shaft, miners' cabin exhibit, and interpretive signs. In its glory days of the late 1800s the mine supported more than 500 people in the boomtown of Cuyamaca City.

General location: Begins at the Cuyamaca Rancho State Park Headquarters, approximately 40 miles east of San Diego.

RIDE 36 *STONEWALL MINE*

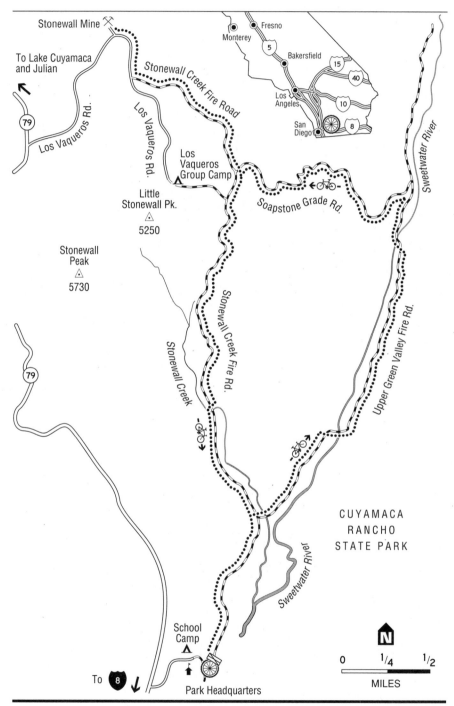

Stonewall Mine

To Lake Cuyamaca
and Julian

79

Los Vaqueros Rd.

Los Vaqueros Rd.

Stonewall Creek Fire Road

Los Vaqueros
Group Camp

Little
Stonewall Pk.
5250

Stonewall
Peak
5730

79

Stonewall Creek

Stonewall Creek Fire Rd.

Soapstone Grade Rd.

Sweetwater River

Upper Green Valley Fire Rd.

CUYAMACA
RANCHO
STATE PARK

Sweetwater River

School
Camp

To 8

Park Headquarters

N

0   ¼   ½
MILES

Monterey
Fresno
5
Bakersfield
15
40
Los Angeles
10
San Diego
8

A view from Stonewall Creek Fire Road.

Elevation change: The ride starts at 4,200' at Upper Green Valley Road and joins Soapstone Grade Road at 4,400'. It then ascends to Stonewall Creek Fire Road at 4,800'. The spur to Stonewall Mine rolls along gently and adds about 100' of climbing to the ride. Total elevation gain: 700'.

Season: Quiet roads and good weather can be found here in the spring and fall.

Services: Water is available at the park headquarters and at Stonewall Mine. You may obtain all services at Lake Cuyamaca, just north of the park on CA 79.

Hazards: The descent on Stonewall Creek Fire Road crosses streambeds containing large loose rocks. You will also encounter some sandy sections of trail.

Rescue index: Help is available near the trailhead at the park headquarters.

Land status: State park.

Maps: A map can be purchased at the headquarters. It is a good guide to trails and fire roads in the park.

Finding the trail: Cuyamaca Rancho State Park is located on CA 79, about 10 miles south of Julian. From San Diego, take Interstate 8 east to the exit for CA 79. Follow CA 79 north for approximately 11 miles to the park headquarters on the right (east) side of the highway. Turn off the highway onto the entrance road for the headquarters. Parking at the headquarters is limited. A good place to park is at the pullout just before the headquarters. As you enter, look for it on the right. This parking area is marked by a plaque embedded in a rock.

Sources of additional information:

Cuyamaca Rancho State Park
12551 Highway 79
Descanso, CA 92016
(619) 765-0755

Notes on the trail: From the recommended parking spot, ride down toward the park headquarters. Before reaching the headquarters you will see a gate and a road on the left that enters Camp Cuyamaca/San Diego School Camp. Go through the gate and follow the road as it swings to the right through the school grounds. Soon the road winds around to the left and becomes dirt. After .5 miles of riding, you come to a gate with a sign for Upper Green Valley Fire Road. Pass through the gate and follow Upper Green Valley Fire Road to the signed Soapstone Grade Road. Turn left and climb on Soapstone Grade Road to an intersection with the signed Stonewall Creek Fire Road. Turn right onto Stonewall Creek Fire Road and follow it to a "T" intersection at paved Los Vaqueros Road. Turn right onto the pavement. Turn right at the next paved road to visit Stonewall Mine. Return the way you came to the intersection of Stonewall Creek Fire Road and Soapstone Grade Road. Continue straight on Stonewall Creek Fire Road, then downhill to Upper Green Valley Road. Turn right on Upper Green Valley Road and ride back to your parked vehicle.

RIDE 37 *CUYAMACA PEAK*

This 9.3-mile loop (with a spur to Cuyamaca Peak) is a great ride if you love to climb. You'll start with 2.7 miles of strenuous uphill pedaling on the one-lane paved Cuyamaca Peak Fire Road. It is punctuated by a few very steep grades (up to 15 percent) and is closed to public motor traffic. Azalea Spring Fire Road and Milk Ranch Road are dirt, two-wheel-drive roads in mostly good condition. There are some rough sections on these dirt roads. The circuit is completed with 1.5 miles of paved cycling on CA 79.

On a clear day, the view from Cuyamaca Peak is incredible. You can see San Diego, the Pacific Ocean, the Salton Sea, and on into Mexico. Azalea Springs Fire Road is a beautiful trail that rolls downhill through deciduous forests and meadows, and past the bubbling Azalea Spring.

General location: Cuyamaca Rancho State Park is approximately 40 miles east of San Diego.
Elevation change: The ride starts at 4,870' and rises steadily to the 6,512' summit of Cuyamaca Peak. Cycling back down, you turn onto Azalea Spring Fire

RIDE 37 *CUYAMACA PEAK*

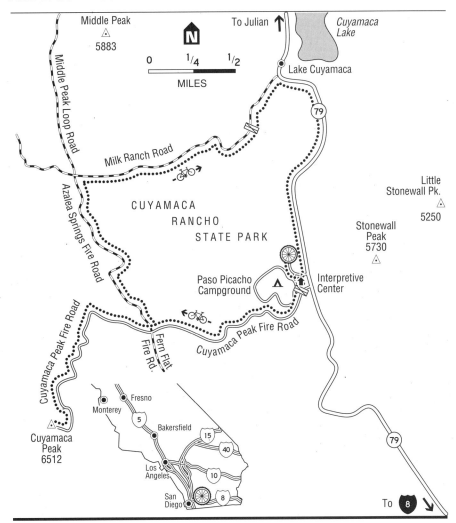

Road at 5,400', and drop to 4,800' at CA 79. Return along the highway back to 4,870'. Total elevation gain: 1,712'.

Season: Spring through late fall. Dress in layers, for you will heat up while climbing to the peak, and it may be windy on top. Summer weekends and holidays can be extremely busy in the park.

Services: Water, restrooms, phone, interpretive information, and camping (including showers) are available at the Paso Picacho Campground. All services can be obtained at Lake Cuyamaca, just north of the park on CA 79.

Hazards: The roads and trails in this park are popular with hikers and equestrians. You may encounter service vehicles on Cuyamaca Peak Fire Road. Be mindful of your speed on the steep, paved descent from the peak. The road is narrow and winding; your view of oncoming traffic is often obstructed. Milk Ranch Road is rock strewn in places.

Rescue index: Help can be found at the Interpretive Center located near the entrance to the Paso Picacho Campground or at the park headquarters. The headquarters is off CA 79 on the left (east) side of the highway, about 3 miles south of the Paso Picacho Campground.

Land status: State park.

Maps: The general map of Cuyamaca Rancho State Park, which can be purchased at the park headquarters, is an excellent guide to this ride.

Finding the trail: Cuyamaca Rancho State Park is located on CA 79, about 10 miles south of Julian. From San Diego follow Interstate 8 east to the exit for CA 79. Follow CA 79 north for approximately 14 miles to the Paso Picacho Campground and Picnic Area on the left (west) side of the highway. Park in the day-use parking area. Park regulations require that you pay a parking fee, and automobiles may not be left overnight.

Sources of additional information:

> Cuyamaca Rancho State Park
> 12551 Highway 79
> Descanso, CA 92016
> (619) 765-0755

Notes on the trail: From the day-use parking area of the Paso Picacho Campground, exit the campground and turn right onto CA 79. Immediately turn right past the Interpretive Center at the "Authorized Vehicles Only" sign. Walk your bike around the locked gate that closes Cuyamaca Peak Fire Road to most traffic. Follow Cuyamaca Peak Fire Road and reach the summit after 3 miles of riding. Return the way you came. After approximately 1.5 miles on the downhill return, turn left onto Azalea Spring Fire Road. It is an easy turn to miss, so watch closely for the signpost as you descend. In another 1.5 miles you come to a "T" intersection at Milk Ranch Road. Turn right onto Milk Ranch Road. This dirt road ends at CA 79. Turn right and follow the highway to the campground and your vehicle.

RIDE 38   OAKZANITA PEAK

This ride combines a short loop with a spur to Oakzanita Peak. It is a 12-mile round-trip. Overall, it is moderately difficult, with the climb to Oakzanita Peak being the most challenging leg. The majority of the riding is on hard-packed dirt roads in good condition. The exception is the two miles of cycling on unpaved South Boundary Fire Road; this stretch is in poor condition with hoof damage and loose rocks. The ride ends with a mile of paved roads in good condition.

Highlighting this trip is the view from Oakzanita Peak. Mule deer are abundant and can often be observed munching in the meadows below the summit. Sightings of golden eagles and red-tailed hawks are common from this 5,054-foot mountain.

General location: Starts at the Green Valley Picnic Area in Cuyamaca Rancho State Park, approximately 40 miles east of San Diego.

Elevation change: The ride begins at 3,957', rises to 4,000' on South Boundary Fire Road, and then drops to 3,800' at CA 79. The route climbs to 4,800' at the end of East Mesa Fire Road near Oakzanita Peak. Hike about .3 miles to reach the summit at 5,054'. Descend back to the highway at 3,800', and then go to 3,957' to complete the trip. Rolling terrain along the course of the ride adds an estimated 100' of climbing to the excursion. Total elevation gain: 1,300' (hike not included).

Season: Visit in the spring or fall for uncrowded trails and nice temperatures.

Services: You will find water and rest rooms at the Green Valley Picnic Area. All services are available at Lake Cuyamaca, just north of the park on CA 79.

Hazards: Watch for equestrians and other trail users. Control your speed on the long descent off Oakzanita Peak. Ride defensively and predictably, especially on CA 79.

Rescue index: Help can be obtained at the park headquarters located approximately 2 miles north of the trailhead on CA 79.

Land status: State park.

Maps: A map can be purchased at the headquarters. It is a good guide to the trails and fire roads in the park.

Finding the trail: Cuyamaca Rancho State Park is located on CA 79, about 10 miles south of Julian. From San Diego, take Interstate 8 east to the exit for CA 79. Follow CA 79 north for about 9 miles to the Green Valley Campground and Picnic Area on the left (west) side of the highway. Turn left and follow the entrance road as it swings right (north). Stop and pay a day-use parking fee at the fee station on the right. Continue in a northerly direction and go past the first campground. Cross the river and proceed south through the second campground to the Green Valley Falls Picnic Area. Park in the day-use lot.

RIDE 38   *OAKZANITA PEAK*

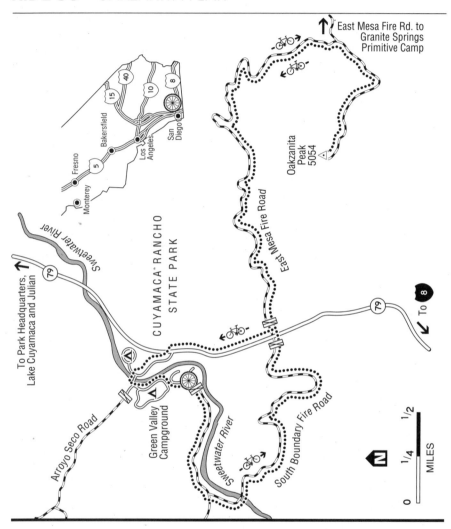

Sources of additional information:

Cuyamaca Rancho State Park
12551 Highway 79
Descanso, CA 92016
(619) 765-0755

Notes on the trail: The trip starts at the gate that blocks the fire road at the Green Valley Falls parking area. Ride down the fire road for nearly 1 mile to an

Crossing Sweetwater River en route to Oakzanita Peak.

intersection with South Boundary Fire Road. Stay to the left and follow South Boundary Fire Road to its end at CA 79. Pick up East Mesa Fire Road directly across the highway. Climb on East Mesa Fire Road for almost 3 miles to an intersection of roads. Turn right (southwest) onto an unmarked spur road where East Mesa Fire Road goes left (northeast) toward the Granite Springs Primitive Camp. Follow the two-track spur road through a grassy meadow to its terminus below Oakzanita Peak. Hike to the top of the mountain. Return the way you came. Turn right onto CA 79 and pedal about .5 miles to the Green Valley Campground and Picnic Area on the left. Turn left and proceed on the entrance road through the campground to your parked vehicle.

RIDE 39 *NOBLE CANYON*

This is a strenuous 13.4-mile loop. The first half of the ride is on Noble Canyon Trail. It is a rocky, rutted, sandy, narrow single-track. Most cyclists will need to push their bikes over portions of this trail. The second half of the loop is on good, hard-packed dirt, two-wheel-drive roads; there is also a short paved stretch. You will descend for the last 5.5 miles of the ride.

Noble Canyon Trail follows Noble Creek as it winds through chaparral, ripar-

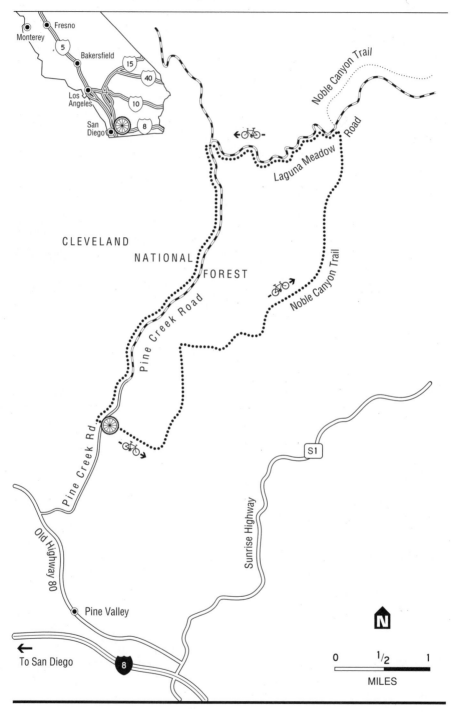

Monterey
Fresno
5
Bakersfield
15
40
10
Los Angeles
San Diego
8

Noble Canyon Trail

Laguna Meadow Road

CLEVELAND

NATIONAL

FOREST

Pine Creek Road

Noble Canyon Trail

Pine Creek Rd.

S1

Sunrise Highway

Old Highway 80

Pine Valley

N

To San Diego

8

0   1/2   1

MILES

Grinnin' and spinnin' in Noble Canyon.

ian woodlands, and forested areas. The creek flows year-round and much of the ride is shaded by large oaks and sycamores. Outstanding views of the Cuyamaca Mountains and the Laguna Mountain Recreation Area make the dirt road descent even more enjoyable.

General location: Begins at the Noble Canyon Trailhead along Pine Creek Road, north of the community of Pine Valley, approximately 45 miles east of San Diego.
Elevation change: The ride starts at 3,740′ and climbs to a high point of 5,250′ near the intersection of Noble Canyon Trail and Laguna Meadow Road. Undulations along the route add about 500′ of climbing to the ride. Total elevation gain: 2,010′.
Season: The spring is a good season for biking in Noble Canyon; it brings comfortable temperatures and an abundance of wildflowers. Cool weather and light trail use make the fall a good choice for a visit. In winter the Laguna Mountains receive more snow than other parts of the Cleveland National Forest.
Services: There is no water on this ride. Water and limited services can be found in the nearby communities of Pine Valley and Guatay. There are pit toilets at the trailhead. All services are available in Alpine (approximately 15 miles west of Noble Canyon on Interstate 8).
Hazards: Surmounting the many obstacles found along Noble Canyon Trail will require intense concentration. Stay alert for people descending on the singletrack; mountain bikers may approach from around blind corners. Poison oak

borders parts of the trail. Rattlesnakes are residents of these mountains. You will be sharing the road portions of this route with motor vehicles. Resist the urge to fly on the downhill, for there may be a car around the next bend.

Rescue index: Help is available in Pine Valley.

Land status: National forest.

Maps: A map of the Noble Canyon National Recreation Trail can be obtained from the Descanso District Office of the Cleveland National Forest in Alpine.

Finding the trail: The trail begins at the parking lot of the Noble Canyon Trailhead. From San Diego, drive east on I-8 for about 40 miles to the off-ramp for Pine Valley. Exit the highway and turn left. Travel north for .3 miles to Old Highway 80. Turn left onto Old Highway 80 and drive 1.2 miles to Pine Creek Road. Turn right (just past the bridge) onto Pine Creek Road and drive 1.6 miles to the trailhead parking area on the right.

Sources of additional information:

> Cleveland National Forest
> Descanso Ranger District
> 3348 Alpine Boulevard
> Alpine, CA 92001-9630
> (619) 445-6235

Notes on the trail: Follow the small signposts that point the way along Noble Canyon Trail. After nearly 3 miles, turn right at the sign directing you toward Laguna Mountain. In another 4.5 miles you come to the unsigned Laguna Meadow Road; this is the first dirt road that you will meet while climbing on Noble Canyon Trail. Turn left onto Laguna Meadow Road as Noble Canyon Trail crosses it. Laguna Meadow Road rolls up and down at first and then descends. Stay on the main road as side roads branch off. Continue downhill as the road becomes the paved Pine Creek Road. The pavement ends in less than 1 mile. At the next few intersections, choose the road that descends. One and one-half miles from the end of the pavement you reach an intersection where both roads descend; turn left to stay on the main road. In another mile you come to pavement again. Follow the pavement and turn left into the Noble Canyon Trailhead parking area.

RIDE 40 *AGUEREBERRY POINT*

This out-and-back, 13-mile round-trip ride takes you into the high desert of Death Valley. The first mile is level and then you begin climbing—gradually for two miles, and then steeply to the top. The return requires good bike handling ability due to the fast and sometimes rough nature of the descent. Except

RIDE 40 *AGUEREBERRY POINT*

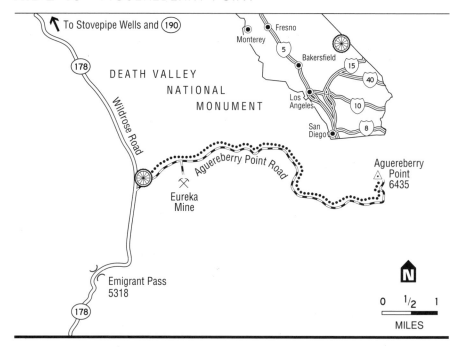

for some washboarding, this hard-packed two-wheel-drive dirt road is in good condition.

At Aguereberry Point you will be rewarded with a panoramic view of Death Valley. Furnace Creek, Devil's Golfcourse, and the snowcapped peaks of the Sierra Nevadas can be seen from this high place in the Panamint Mountains. On the way back, a short side trip will take you to the Eureka Mine and remnants of a once-thriving mining town. Pete "Pierre" Aguereberry and Shorty Harris discovered gold here in 1905. Pete worked the mine until his death in 1945. He took pleasure in taking tourists up to see the fine view of Death Valley. Pete Aguereberry built the road himself—hence, Aguereberry Point Road.

General location: Begins 20 miles south of Stove Pipe Wells, Death Valley.
Elevation change: This trip begins at 4,885' and climbs to a high point of 6,435' at Aguereberry Point. Total elevation gain: 1,550'.
Season: The late fall through spring is the best time to ride in Death Valley. The high elevation of this route makes for comfortable temperatures, especially when compared to conditions found on the valley floor. Traffic is usually light because of the road's distance from the main Visitor Center at Furnace Creek.

Part of the view from Aguereberry Point.

Services: There is no water on this ride. All services are available in the town of Stove Pipe Wells.

Hazards: Special care should be taken when approaching bends in the road. Motorists will not be looking for cyclists and may be driving fast. Be prepared for sudden changes in the weather. Wear sunscreen and carry lots of water.

Rescue index: Help can be obtained in Stove Pipe Wells.

Land status: National monument.

Maps: A map of Death Valley National Monument is available at the Visitor Center in Furnace Creek. It is a good guide to this ride.

Finding the trail: From Lone Pine take US 395 south to CA 136. Follow CA 136 east for 19 miles to CA 190. Continue straight toward Death Valley as CA 136 becomes CA 190. Drive 51 miles on CA 190 to its intersection with Wildrose Road (CA 178). Turn right (south) onto Wildrose Road (CA 178) and travel approximately 13 miles to Aguereberry Point Road on the left (east) side of the road. Turn left and drive 100 yards to park in the turnout on the right.

Sources of additional information:

Death Valley Visitor Center
Furnace Creek
Death Valley, CA 92328
(619) 786-2331

Notes on the trail: Follow Aguereberry Point Road to the turnaround spot at

RIDE 41 *MOVIE ROAD*

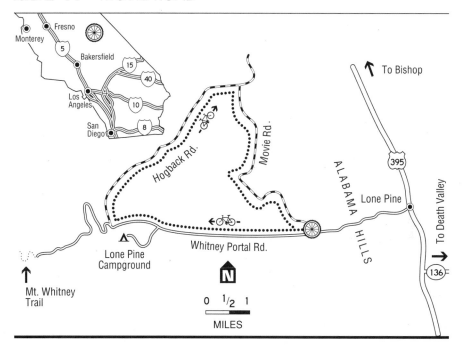

To Bishop

Fresno
Monterey
Bakersfield
Los Angeles
San Diego
To Death Valley
Movie Rd.
Hogback Rd.
ALABAMA HILLS
Lone Pine
Lone Pine Campground
Whitney Portal Rd.
Mt. Whitney Trail

N

0 1/2 1
MILES

Aguereberry Point. On the return, about 1 mile from the parking area, Eureka Mine can be seen on the hillside to your left. Turn left to check out the mine. It is well worth a visit.

RIDE 41 *MOVIE ROAD*

Strong cyclists with intermediate bike handling skills will enjoy this scenic 17.5-mile loop. The 5.6-mile climb on paved Whitney Portal Road is moderately difficult, with some steep sections in the last two miles. Hogback Road is mostly downhill and level to the intersection with Movie Road. Movie Road climbs moderately for about two miles and then rolls up and down, steeply at times, to the end of the ride. Hogback and Movie Roads are unpaved two-wheel-drive roads in fair to good condition; both contain washboarded and sandy areas.

The view of Mt. Whitney and Lone Pine Peak from Whitney Portal Road is outstanding. A close look may reveal hang gliders skimming the mountain tops. The descent on Hogback Road is invigorating; it starts out fast and then mel-

The Sierra Mountains and Whitney Portal Road.

lows into a cruise that goes on and on. Surrounded by the huge red rocks that line Movie Road, it is easy to see why this was a choice location for the filming of television and movie westerns.

General location: Begins at the intersection of Whitney Portal Road and Movie Road, 2.7 miles west of Lone Pine.

Elevation change: Start the ride on Whitney Portal Road at 4,490' and reach the ride's high point of 6,560' at the intersection with Hogback Road. From here you drop 1,970' to meet Movie Road at 4,590'. Movie Road climbs gradually to 4,920' and then falls to 4,490' back at the trailhead. An estimated 200' is gained on the ups and downs along Movie Road. Total elevation gain: 2,600'.

Season: Late fall through spring. It is possible to ride here year-round, but high summer temperatures can make riding unpleasant and even dangerous. The weather can be unpredictable; carry sunscreen, raingear, and extra clothing.

Services: There is no water on this ride, so fill up in town. If more water is needed, a side trip into the Lone Pine Campground is recommended. About 4 miles into the ride, turn left off Whitney Portal Road and follow an entrance road about 1 mile to the Lone Pine Campground and piped water. All services are available in Lone Pine.

Hazards: Whitney Portal Road sees a moderate amount of traffic, and vehicles travel at high speeds. There is no shoulder, so watch yourself. There are some sandy sections on Hogback and Movie Roads. After riding on Movie Road for 3 miles you will encounter a steep descent with loose material at the bottom; control your speed.

Rescue index: Help can be found in Lone Pine.

Land status: National forest and Bureau of Land Management lands.

Maps: USGS 7.5 minute quadrangle maps: Lone Pine, Independence, and Mt. Pinchot.

Finding the trail: From the stoplight on US 395 in Lone Pine, head west on Whitney Portal Road and follow it 2.7 miles to the intersection with Movie Road. Park in the large dirt parking area on the right.

Sources of additional information:

Inyo National Forest
Mt. Whitney Ranger District
640 South Main Street
Lone Pine, CA 93545
(619) 876-5542

Notes on the trail: Pedal west on the paved Whitney Portal Road. After cycling for 5.6 miles, before the first major switchback on Whitney Portal Road and just before a sign reading "Trailers Not Recommended," turn right onto the unsigned Hogback Road. Hogback Road is paved at first, but soon turns to dirt and curves around to the right as you begin a long descent. Follow the main road for 6 miles to a "T" intersection at signed Movie Road. Turn right onto Movie Road. Three and one-half miles of riding on Movie Road will bring you to a narrow outcropping of rocks near some willows. The route passes between the rocks. About .5 miles beyond the outcropping, the main road curves hard to the left and a side road continues straight. Follow the main road left. Reach your parked vehicle after another 1.6 miles.

RIDE 42 *MAZOURKA CANYON*

This 22.2-mile ride through Mazourka Canyon is an out-and-back trip with a short loop around Santa Rita Flat. Although the ascent is moderately steep, the cycling is made more difficult due to the length of the climb (nine miles!) and the condition of the road surface. Mazourka Canyon Road is a two-wheel-drive gravel road in fair condition, with some washboarding and loose rocks. The road around Santa Rita Flat is in better condition, but you do cross some sandy washes and rocky areas. This road is nearly level as it winds around the flat.

Mazourka Canyon is barren and dry, but the scenery improves as you gain altitude. At Santa Rita Flat you get a beautiful view across the Owens Valley to the rugged peaks of the Sierras. Santa Rita Flat is a well-used cattle grazing area, as evidenced by a corral, a hoof-muddied spring, and an abundance of cow pies in the road. This ride is a good "workout," if an extended moderate climb is what you're looking for. The descent is fast and long, but the fun factor is diminished by the bumpiness of the road.

RIDE 42 *MAZOURKA CANYON*

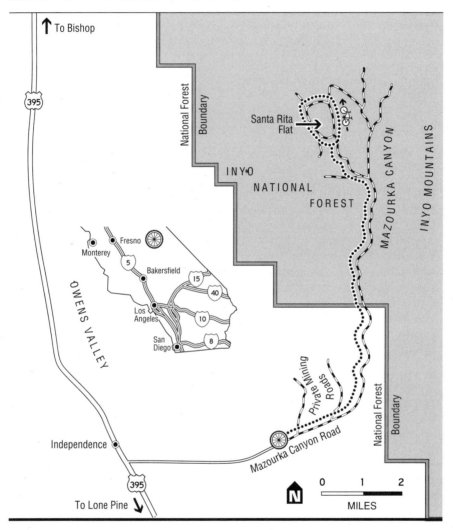

General location: The ride begins east of the community of Independence, at the end of the pavement on Mazourka Canyon Road (approximately 40 miles south of Bishop).

Elevation change: You start at 4,000' and climb to a high point of 6,800' at Santa Rita Flat. Total elevation gain: 2,800'.

Season: Spring is the most beautiful time of year to ride in the Inyo Mountains. Summer temperatures can soar, so ride in the early morning. Snow is common in the winter at higher elevations.

Descending on Mazourka Canyon Road.

Services: There is no water on this ride. All services are available in Independence.

Hazards: Stay alert for cattleguards, sand, rocks, and washboarding on the return descent.

Rescue index: Help can be found in Independence.

Land status: National forest and Bureau of Land Management lands.

Maps: USGS 7.5 minute quadrangle map: Independence.

Finding the trail: Follow US 395 south from Bishop for approximately 40 miles to Independence. Turn left (east) onto Mazourka Canyon Road and follow it for 4.4 miles to the end of the pavement. Park your vehicle on the right side of the road.

Sources of additional information:

Inyo National Forest
White Mountain Ranger District
798 North Main Street
Bishop, CA 93514
(619) 873-4207

Notes on the trail: Begin this trip at the end of the pavement on Mazourka Canyon Road. Follow Mazourka Canyon Road as it swings north and passes a mining road on the left. You will pass an Inyo National Forest Boundary sign after 4.6 miles of riding. Continue up the canyon for another 3.4 miles to a

"Y" intersection at a sign for Santa Rita Flat/Badger Flat. Turn left toward Santa Rita Flat. Stay to the right as the road circles around Santa Rita Flat. Pursue the main road and pedal past a corral. About 1 mile beyond the corral you will reach a "T" intersection. Turn left at this intersection and proceed downhill toward Santa Rita Spring. As you approach the spring you will pass through a sandy wash. Immediately after climbing out of the wash, you arrive at an intersection of trails. Turn left (south) here onto a two-track road and ride past the cattle watering hole that is Santa Rita Spring. Follow this two-track to meet the road you came in on. Return the way you came.

RIDE 43 *BOOLE TREE*

This is an easy, five-mile round-trip out-and-back excursion to the Boole Tree Trailhead. A pleasant one-mile walk takes you to the third largest Sequoia in the world. The ride to the hiking trail is mostly downhill, with a couple of easy to moderate ascents and one short, steep climb. The return is mostly easy to moderately difficult climbing. The tour is on an unpaved, two-wheel-drive road in good condition.

The route travels through a dense yellow pine forest. Near the start of the ride you will pass some beautifully symmetrical conifers. They look like large cedars, but are actually century-old Sequoias. After two miles you'll pedal through Stump Meadow. It is littered with massive logs and stumps—remnants of early logging operations. Wildflowers thrive in the open environment left by the lumberjacks.

Less accessible than some other giant Sequoias, Boole Tree offers a unique and perhaps more appropriate encounter with an ancient redwood. Boole Tree's more popular relatives, like the General Sherman Tree, are sightseeing attractions that draw large crowds. It does not matter that Boole Tree is not the very largest Sequoia; it is huge, awe inspiring, and has been left to grow and be admired in a natural setting.

General location: The route follows Forest Service Road 13S55 as it meanders through the Sequoia National Forest, approximately 65 miles east of Fresno.
Elevation change: From 6,850' at the start of the ride, you drop to a low point of 6,200'. The parking area for the Boole Tree Trail is at 6,240'; the tree is at 6,500'. Undulations over the course of the route add an estimated 100' of climbing to the ride. Total elevation gain: 790' (hike not included).
Season: Good wildflower displays and light use make the late spring a pleasant time for cycling here. The forest is busy on summer weekends and holidays with Fresnoians seeking cooler temperatures in the mountains. The highway into this portion of the Sequoia National Forest is closed in winter.

RIDE 43 *BOOLE TREE*

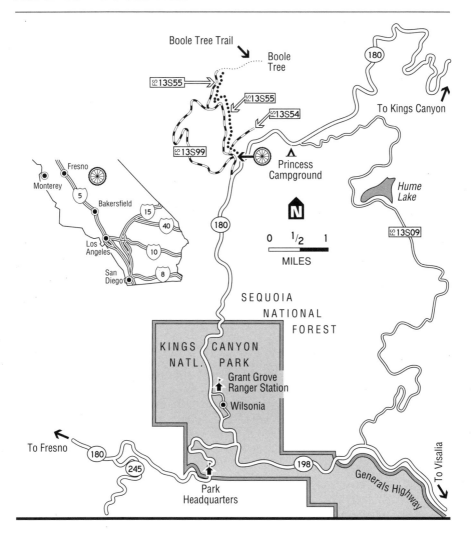

Services: There is no water on this ride. Piped water can be obtained seasonally at the nearby Princess Campground. In summer you will find food, lodging, telephones, and limited groceries at the Hume Lake Christian Camp. All services are available in Fresno.

Hazards: FS 13S55 sees a fair amount of vehicular traffic. The road is narrow in places and has some blind corners.

Rescue index: Help can be found in Wilsonia in Kings Canyon National Park on CA 180.

The magnificent Boole Tree.

Land status: National forest.

Maps: A map of the Sequoia National Forest may be obtained at the Hume Lake Ranger Station. This station is located outside the National Forest Boundary, approximately 30 miles east of Fresno on CA 180.

Finding the trail: From Fresno, travel east on CA 180. After driving approximately 55 miles, you will enter the General Grant Grove Section of the Kings Canyon National Park. Stay on CA 180 and pass through Wilsonia and out of the park. Go about 7 miles beyond Wilsonia to the Sequoia National Forest Princess Campground on the right. The campground is well signed and easy to find. You can fill up with water here and then return the way you came on CA 180 (head west) for 1.8 miles to reach FS 13S55 on the right (north) side of the highway. It is marked with a small sign that is difficult to see from the highway (especially when eastbound). Drive up FS 13S55 for about .5 miles to an intersection of roads and park your vehicle. Do not block access to the roads.

Sources of additional information:

Sequoia National Forest
Hume Lake Ranger District
36273 East Kings Canyon Road
Dunlap, CA 93621
(209) 338-2251

Notes on the trail: Take signed FS 13S55 towards Boole Tree. Follow the main road to reach the parking area for Boole Tree Trail. The hike to the giant Sequoia is a two-mile round-trip. Return the way you came.

Those not accustomed to the thin air found at higher elevations may find this trip to be more difficult than expected.

RIDE 44 *FOREST SERVICE ROAD 13S05 / SEQUOIA NATIONAL FOREST*

This 16.6-mile round-trip out-and-back ride takes you through some wonderful redwood groves and to some great views of the Monarch Divide. The ride to the turnaround point is a long, moderately difficult ascent, punctuated by some short steep hills. The first one-quarter mile is strenuous, and then the climbing gets easier. The majority of the route is over a four-wheel-drive, hard-packed dirt road in good condition. You will encounter some short stretches that are rocky, bumpy, and rutted; these sections of road are technically demanding.

After riding for 5.5 miles, you come to a magnificent vista. At the roadside the mountain drops off steeply, leaving you with a grand view of Monarch Divide. The gray and bluish rock faces of this geologic formation are striking. Spanish Mountain and Obelisk can be seen high up; below is the Monarch Wilderness Area bordering the South Fork of the Kings River.

This outing takes you through several stands of the mightiest trees in the world—the giant Sequoias of the High Sierra. Although shorter than coastal redwoods, Sierra redwoods (Sequoia gigantum) have enormous diameters, some reaching up to 40 feet. The trip back down is fast and fun. You may wish to conclude your ride with a refreshing swim in nearby Hume Lake.

General location: Starts near Hume Lake in the Sequoia National Forest, approximately 70 miles east of Fresno.

Elevation change: The ride begins at 5,300' and climbs to a high point of 6,600' on Forest Service Road 13S05. Total elevation gain: 1,300'.

Season: Late spring through early fall. Cool temperatures at higher elevations make this a nice place to ride in the summer. The only access road, CA 180, is closed in winter.

Services: There is no water on this ride. Piped water can be obtained seasonally at the nearby Hume Lake and Princess Campgrounds. Food, lodging, telephones, and limited groceries can be found at the Hume Lake Christian Camp during the summer. All services are available in Fresno.

Hazards: Portions of the ride traverse rocky terrain. Watch for loose rocks, ruts, and sandy sections. Anticipate other recreationists, including motorists. Control your speed on the descent. Expect sudden weather changes.

Rescue index: Help is available at the Hume Lake Christian Camp.

RIDE 44 *FOREST SERVICE ROAD 13S05 / SEQUOIA NATIONAL FOREST*

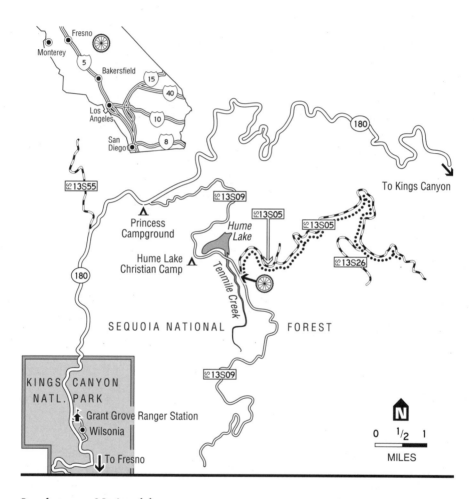

Land status: National forest.

Maps: A map of the Sequoia National Forest may be obtained at the Hume Lake Ranger Station. This station lies outside the National Forest Boundary; it is located approximately 30 miles east of Fresno on CA 180.

Finding the trail: From Fresno, travel east on CA 180. After approximately 55 miles you will enter the General Grant Grove Section of the Kings Canyon National Park. Stay on CA 180 and pass through Wilsonia and out of the park. Drive about 7 miles beyond Wilsonia to a small sign for Hume Lake; the sign for

Riding among the giants.

Hume Lake and the road down to the lake are just beyond the Sequoia National Forest Princess Campground. Turn right onto Hume Lake Road and proceed downhill. Follow the signs to the Hume Lake Christian Camp. Continue past the Hume Lake Christian Camp as the road takes you around the lake and past some summer homes. Go over the bridge that crosses Ten Mile Creek and continue on the main road where a side road leads left to public beaches. Drive uphill .5 miles beyond the bridge to the signed FS 13S05 on the left. There is room to park one small vehicle at the start of FS 13S05. You can park also in a large turnout a little farther uphill on the paved road.

Sources of additional information:

Sequoia National Forest
Hume Lake Ranger District
36273 East Kings Canyon Road
Dunlap, CA 93621
(209) 338-2251

Notes on the trail: The ride starts at the small sign for FS 13S05. After riding for 1.2 miles you reach a "Y" intersection; stay right and follow the main road. Well into the ride, 7 miles from the start, a secondary road enters from the right. Continue straight on the main road. We turned around after 8.3 miles of pedaling; you may wish to explore farther along this road. Return the way you came.

RIDE 45   *COYOTE RIDGE*

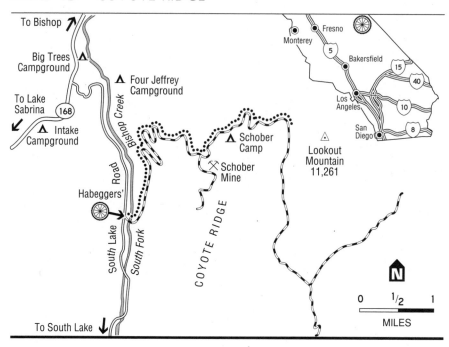

To Bishop

Big Trees
Campground

Four Jeffrey
Campground

To Lake
Sabrina   168

Intake
Campground

Bishop Creek

South Lake Road

South Fork

Habeggers'

Schober
Camp

Schober
Mine

COYOTE RIDGE

Lookout
Mountain
11,261

To South Lake

Monterey   Fresno

Bakersfield

Los
Angeles

San
Diego

5   15   40   10   8

N

0   ¹/₂   1

MILES

RIDE 45   *COYOTE RIDGE*

RIDE 45   COYOTE RIDGE

This technical, 11-mile out-and-back will challenge and delight experienced mountain bikers. The 5.5-mile climb to the turnaround point is steep; loose rocks and sand complicate matters. This dirt double-track was once an access route for miners working claims on Coyote Ridge. It is now in disrepair and closed to motor vehicles.

Cyclists tackling this demanding ride are rewarded with the barren alpine beauty of Coyote Ridge and magnificent views. At the crest of the trail, scramble up the lichen-covered rocks and have a look around. To the west are the rugged peaks of the John Muir Wilderness. Prominent are Mt. Humphreys, Mt. Tom, Basin Mountain, and Mt. Emerson, all over 13,000 feet high.

General location: Coyote Ridge is a plateau that lies southwest of Bishop and east of the main Sierras. The ride begins along the south fork of Bishop Creek in the Inyo National Forest, approximately 17 miles southwest of Bishop.

Looking north from Coyote Ridge.

Elevation change: The road up to the ridge begins at 8,500′ and climbs to a high point of 11,000′ near Lookout Mountain. A short hike will take you to the summit of Lookout Mountain at 11,261′. Total elevation gain: 2,500′ (hike not included).

Season: Late spring through early fall. Summer temperatures can be cool due to the high elevation of the ride. Weather changes can be sudden; carry raingear and warm clothing.

Services: There is no water on this ride. Four Jeffrey Campground, located approximately 1.5 miles north of the trailhead on South Lake Road, has piped water. All services can be obtained in Bishop.

Hazards: The road is rocky, sandy, and rutted in places. Control your speed on the downhill return; walk your bike if necessary. The route is exposed and is a dangerous place in a thunderstorm.

Rescue index: Help is available in Bishop.

Land status: National forest.

Maps: USGS 7.5 minute quadrangle maps: Mt. Tom, Bishop, and Mt. Goddard.

Finding the trail: From Bishop, follow CA 168 southwest into Bishop Creek Canyon for approximately 15 miles. Turn left onto South Lake Road (at a sign for Four Jeffrey Campground). Follow the road for about 2 miles to Habegger's and Bishop Creek Lodge. The ride begins .2 miles south of Habegger's. Look for the dirt road paralleling the main road; you can see it climbing up the east side of the canyon. Park on the shoulder of South Lake Road or along the dirt road at the start of the ride. Do not block the road.

Sources of additional information:

Inyo National Forest
White Mountain Ranger District
798 North Main Street
Bishop, CA 93514
(619) 873-4207

Notes on the trail: The ride starts at the unnamed dirt road to Schober Mining Camp. Cross the creek over a small bridge. Just beyond the bridge the road swings north and you start climbing. After 3.4 miles you reach an unmarked intersection. Turn left and ride another .6 miles to Schober Camp. Continue past Schober Camp for 1.5 miles to the turnaround point at a saddle near the top of Lookout Mountain. Return the way you came.

RIDE 46 *ELDERBERRY CANYON / WELLS MEADOW*

This is a loop ride with an out-and-back spur to a corral in Wells Meadow. It is a relatively easy, 18-mile trip. It is made more difficult by poor road conditions, especially the first three miles which are over a rocky, four-wheel-drive road. The road does improve, but still contains some rocks, as well as sandy sections. This rough stretch is followed by several miles of pedaling on paved roads. The one-way spur to Wells Meadow is on unpaved roads that are sandy and washboarded in places. Backtracking from the meadow, you rejoin the loop and follow pavement to complete the ride.

This is a good circuit for cyclists of all abilities who want to acclimatize themselves to the altitude of the Bishop area. Though much of the ride is on pavement, the roads are lightly traveled and take you through a pleasant countryside setting of farms and ranchlands. Lovely views of the nearby Sierras are an added bonus.

General location: Starts from the Horton Creek Campground, approximately 10 miles north of Bishop.

Elevation change: Begin the ride at 4,980' and drop to 4,880' in the first mile. This is followed by a climb to 5,150' and then a descent to 4,600' near Rovana. The high point of the ride is 5,200' at Wells Meadow. Return across Round Valley to 4,700', and then pedal uphill for 1 mile to your vehicle at 4,980'. Total elevation gain: 1,150'.

Season: Year-round. Summer temperatures can get high, so ride in the early morning. In the spring you can enjoy comfortable temperatures and wildflowers along the roadsides. Snow cover is likely in the winter months. This area is the

RIDE 46 *ELDERBERRY CANYON / WELLS MEADOW*

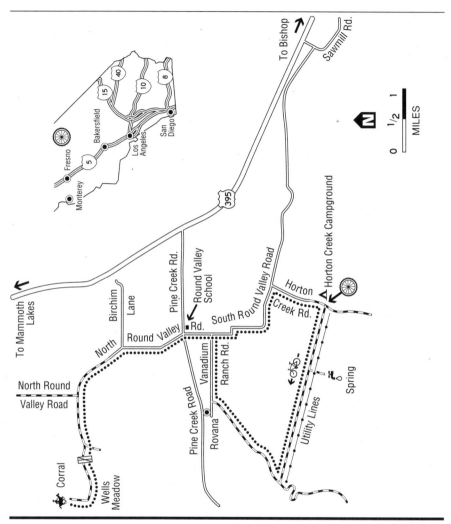

winter range for the Sherwin deer herd. It is not uncommon to see hundreds of deer browsing in Elderberry Canyon and Wells Meadow from December to April.

Services: There is no water on this ride. All services can be obtained in Bishop.

Hazards: Control your speed on the dirt road descents and watch for sandy spots. There are no shoulders on the paved roads. You will cross a cattleguard near the end of the ride.

Always take your favorite mechanic along.

Rescue index: Help is available in Bishop.
Land status: National forest and Bureau of Land Management lands.
Maps: USGS 7.5 minute quadrangle map: Mt. Tom.
Finding the trail: Follow US 395 north from Bishop for 6 miles and turn left onto Sawmill Road. Follow Sawmill Road for .2 miles and turn right onto South Round Valley Road. Drive for 4 miles on South Round Valley Road to Horton Creek Road on the left. Turn left toward the Horton Creek Campground. After 1 mile, you come to a dirt road on the right that parallels some overhead utility lines. Park in a campsite space if you intend to camp or on the side of the dirt road. Do not block the road.

Sources of additional information:

Bureau of Land Management
873 North Main Street, Suite 201
Bishop, CA 93514

Inyo National Forest
White Mountain Ranger District
798 North Main Street
Bishop, CA 93514
(619) 873-4207

Notes on the trail: From the Horton Creek Campground, follow the dirt road west. You will be paralleling overhead utility lines and going downhill. In 1 mile, continue straight where a double-track goes left toward a spring. After 2 more miles of riding, turn right (northeast) at a crossroad. The road takes you downhill toward the community of Rovana. After 1.5 miles, you will ride through a littered area and past some junked cars. Soon the road turns to pavement and you come to a "T" intersection. Turn right onto the unsigned Vanadium Ranch Road. After a little more than 1 mile on Vanadium Ranch Road you come to another "T" intersection. Turn left onto the signed North Round Valley Road. Pass the Round Valley School and cross Pine Creek Road to stay on North Round Valley Road. Go by Birchim Lane on the right in another mile. Continue straight as the pavement ends. Follow the dirt road for 1 mile and continue straight toward the mountains where the main road goes right. In another mile you reach a "Y" intersection; stay right on the main road and ride a short distance to a locked gate. Pass your bike over the gate. Travel up the road and cycle through Wells Meadow to a corral at the end of the road. Return the way you came to the intersection of North Round Valley Road and Vanadium Ranch Road. Go straight on North Round Valley Road. Continue straight as North Round Valley Road becomes South Round Valley Road. Turn right onto Horton Creek Road and proceed through the Horton Creek Campground to your vehicle.

RIDE 47 *ANCIENT BRISTLECONE*

This 26-mile round-trip out-and-back is long, hard, and technically demanding. Grades that would seem easy at sea level will leave you gasping at 10,000 feet. There are several long, steep grinds in both directions and the road surface is rocky and washboarded. The condition of the unpaved, two-wheel-drive road varies from good to poor. There are even some dangerously rocky and bumpy sections.

At this elevation the White Mountains are stark and desolate. The forest is

RIDE 47 *ANCIENT BRISTLECONE*

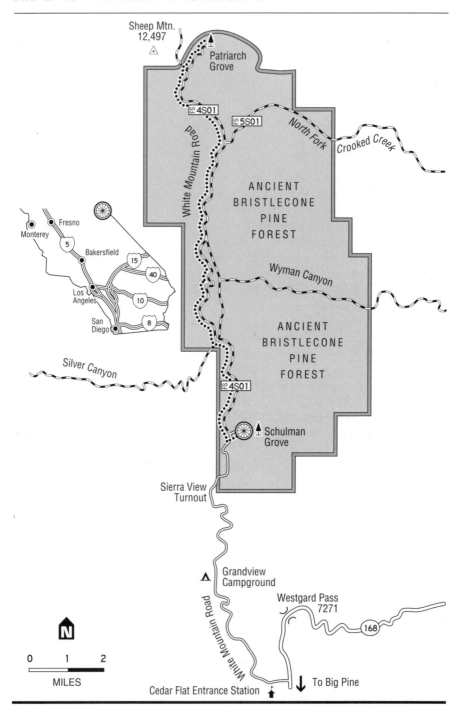

The road to Patriarch Grove.

composed of pockets of wind-battered trees and expansive alpine meadows. Its harsh and barren character is extremely beautiful. The feeling is one of openness; the air is clean and clear, the sunlight intense. After approximately four miles of riding you reach a viewpoint. Here you can see west into the interior of the Sierras to glaciers, meadows, and snowcapped peaks.

In this part of the Inyo National Forest you can walk among the oldest living things on earth—bristlecone pines. Some of these trees have been alive for over 45 centuries. Think of it! There is an Information Center and two self-guided trails at the Schulman Grove. The Patriarch Grove, the turnaround point, also has a self-guided trail.

General location: Begins at the Schulman Grove in the Ancient Bristlecone Pine Forest, approximately 25 miles northeast of Big Pine.
Elevation change: The ride starts at 10,100' and climbs to a high point of 11,200' at the Patriarch Grove. Add an estimated 1,000' of additional climbing in each direction for the undulating nature of this ride. Total elevation gain: 3,100'.
Season: Late spring through early fall. The Ancient Bristlecone Pine Forest is normally open from June through October; call the Forest Service to check on closings. Be prepared for unpredictable weather. Thunderstorms can occur without warning and snow is a threat in the spring and fall.
Services: There is no water to be found east of Big Pine; bring all that you will

need. There are no gas stations east of Big Pine. All services can be obtained in Big Pine and Bishop.

Hazards: There are some inherent dangers that should be considered when riding at high elevations. These include sudden drops in temperature, high winds, thunderstorms, and the possibility of altitude sickness. Dehydration can also be a problem; bring plenty of water and drink often. Wear sunscreen and sunglasses to protect against intense ultraviolet rays. Although you have gained elevation overall upon reaching the Patriarch Grove, you will encounter almost as much climbing on the return. Much of the return riding is difficult, especially since you are already fatigued. The roads are rock strewn and contain long stretches that are washboarded. Steep descents over this terrain can be treacherous for tired riders or those lacking adequate bike handling skills. Vehicular traffic is light but moves along rapidly, creating dust and kicking up small rocks. There is no shelter along the route. Turn around if the weather becomes threatening or if problems develop.

Rescue index: Help may be available at the Information Center at the Schulman Grove. This center is staffed by rangers during regular business hours. Stop in before embarking on the ride and check on their hours of operation. The next closest help is in Big Pine. Traffic is light. Plan on being completely self-sufficient.

Land status: National forest.

Maps: The Inyo National Forest Map, available at ranger stations, is a good guide to this ride. The Information Center at the Schulman Grove has several useful maps for sale.

Finding the trail: From US 395 in Big Pine, travel east on CA 168. Drive for 13 miles on CA 168 and turn left on White Mountain Road at a sign for the White Mountain Bristlecone Forest. Follow White Mountain Road in a northerly direction past the Cedar Flats Entrance Station, the Grandview Campground, and the Sierra View Turnout. Go 2 miles beyond the Sierra View Turnout to the Schulman Grove on the right. Park your vehicle in the Schulman Grove parking lot.

Sources of additional information:

Inyo National Forest
White Mountain Ranger District
798 North Main Street
Bishop, CA 93514
(619) 873-4207

Notes on the trail: From the Schulman Grove parking lot, turn right onto White Mountain Road (Forest Service Road 4S01). The pavement ends almost immediately and you pass a sign that reads "Patriarch Grove—12 miles." (We found it to be closer to 13 miles.) After 3 miles, you pass an intersection and a road that leads left to Silver Canyon Laws and right to Wyman Canyon Deep Spring. There are 2 mileage signs here; one points to Patriarch Grove and reads "7 miles" (wrong again; it's more like 10 miles). The other points back to Schulman Grove and reads "2 miles" (wrong a third time, for it's more like 3 miles). Continue straight toward the Patriarch Grove. In 1 mile you reach a parking area with views to the west. From this viewpoint it's about 3 miles to an intersection where a road goes hard to the right, to Wyman Canyon. Stay to the left toward the Patriarch Grove. Ride 2.6 miles further to another intersection where FS 5S01 goes right to Crooked Creek Station and Cottonwood Creek. Continue straight toward the Patriarch Grove; the sign reads "Patriarch Grove—3.5 miles" (correct!). Cycle 2.5 miles to a "**Y**" intersection and a sign directing you right to Patriarch Grove. Travel 1 more mile to reach the Patriarch Grove parking area. Bicycles are not permitted on the nature trail. Return the way you came.

RIDE 48   *RED CANYON / CHIDAGO CANYON*

This is a relatively easy, 18-mile round-trip out-and-back ride. The route follows a good two-wheel-drive dirt road. One-and-one-half miles into the trip there is a short, moderately steep hill; then it is mostly downhill to the turnaround point. The return is an easy to moderately difficult ascent.

Forefathers of the Paiute Indians once roamed here. They left behind many carvings on nearby rock outcroppings. The Red Rock Petroglyphs can be explored 3.5 miles into the ride. This group is known for its many examples of human hand and footprints, and large animal tracks. At Chidago Canyon you will find the Chidago Canyon Petroglyphs. This group's nickname, "Newspaper Rock," is derived from the pictures being so numerous and crowded together.

General location: Begins on Chidago Canyon Road, approximately 19 miles north of Bishop on US 6.
Elevation change: The ride starts at 4,500′, climbs to 4,600′ in 2.2 miles, and then descends gradually to 4,200′ at the Chidago Canyon Petroglyphs. Total elevation gain: 500′.
Season: The riding here is best in the spring, fall, and winter. Set out in the early morning if you are planning on a summer visit.
Services: There is no water on this ride. All services can be obtained in Bishop.
Hazards: Control your speed on the moderately steep descent near the end of the ride. The road surface contains some loose gravel here, and there are deep, silty patches at the bottom of the hill. This is an exposed ride through the desert; be prepared to help yourself out of any trouble that might arise. Travel with others and carry plenty of water.
Rescue index: Help is available in Bishop.
Land status: Bureau of Land Management lands.
Maps: The Inyo National Forest map that can be purchased at ranger stations is a good guide to this route. You may wish to pick up the "Petroglyph Loop

RIDE 48 *RED CANYON / CHIDAGO CANYON*

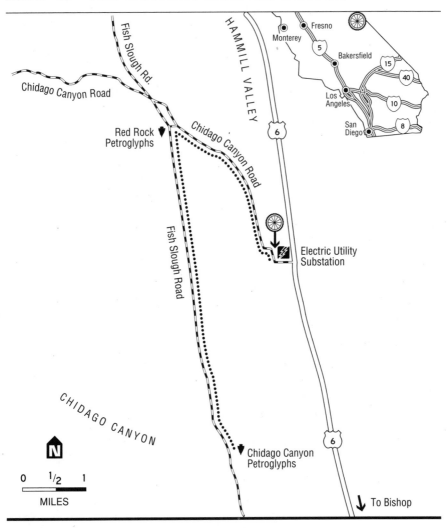

Trip" handout that is available at the White Mountain Ranger District Office in Bishop.

Finding the trail: In Bishop, at the intersection of US 395 and US 6, travel north on US 6. Drive for 19 miles to Chidago Canyon Road on the left (west) side of the highway. Turn left and follow the gravel road past the electric utility substation. Continue downhill as the road curves right (north) and park on the right side of the road.

Chidago Canyon Petroglyphs.

Sources of additional information:

Inyo National Forest
White Mountain Ranger District
798 North Main Street
Bishop, CA 93514
(619) 873-4207

Notes on the trail: Begin the ride on Chidago Canyon Road and follow it in a northerly direction. After 3.2 miles, you come to an intersection; turn left toward a rock outcropping. In .2 miles you reach another intersection that is directly across from the rock outcropping (Red Canyon Petroglyphs). Turn left here onto unsigned Fish Slough Road. Ride for approximately 5.5 miles on Fish Slough

Road to reach the Chidago Canyon Petroglyphs on the left at a chain-link fence. Return the way you came.

RIDE 49 SAWMILL ROAD / INYO CRATERS

This is a 16-mile loop, with a one-way spur to Inyo Craters. It is an easy to moderately difficult circuit, depending on your physical conditioning and acclimation to high altitude. All of the roads, paved and unpaved, are in good condition.

This is a good ride for getting acquainted with the Mammoth Lakes area. Sawmill Road climbs through a shady conifer forest with some mountain views opening up as you approach US 395. At Inyo Craters there is an interpretive sign detailing the Craters' formation during some recent volcanic activity. On Scenic Loop Road you gain good views of Mammoth Mountain and the Sierra Crest before a fun descent back into town.

General location: Begins near the Inyo National Forest Shady Rest Campground in the town of Mammoth Lakes, approximately 40 miles north of Bishop.
Elevation change: The trip starts on Sawmill Road at 7,760' and crests at 8,000' at Mammoth Knoll. Then the route descends to meet Mammoth Scenic Loop Road at 7,600'. The turnoff to Inyo Craters is at 8,080', and the craters themselves are at 8,240'. You will descend back to 8,080' and then climb to a high point of 8,300'. This is followed by a descent back to the entrance of the campground at 7,710'. The loop is completed back at the start of Sawmill Road at 7,760'. Total elevation gain (including hike): 1,150'.
Season: Late spring through early fall. The weather may change rapidly; be prepared with extra clothing.
Services: There is no water on this ride. Piped water can be found seasonally at the Shady Rest Campground and at the Shady Rest Park. All services can be obtained in Mammoth Lakes.
Hazards: All of the roads in this ride description see traffic from motor vehicles. Be especially careful on Scenic Loop Road and CA 203. There is an intermittent shoulder on Scenic Loop Road. Control your speed on the descent into Mammoth Lakes.
Rescue index: Help is available in Mammoth Lakes.
Land status: National forest.
Maps: The "Bicycle Routes—Mammoth Lakes, California" brochure/map is a good guide to this ride. It is available at the Mammoth Lakes Visitor Information Center on Main Street (CA 203) in Mammoth Lakes.
Finding the trail: From US 395, take the Mammoth Lakes turnoff. Travel west on CA 203. After 3 miles you will pass the U.S. Forest Service Visitor Center on the right (it's worth a stop). Just west of the Visitor Center on CA 203 is

RIDE 49 *SAWMILL ROAD / INYO CRATERS*

the entrance road for Shady Rest Campground on the right. Turn right and follow this road north toward Shady Rest Campground. Continue past the campground. You will reach the end of the pavement at a parking area for Shady Rest Park. Park your vehicle here.

Sources of additional information:

Inyo National Forest
Mammoth Ranger District

Inyo Craters.

P.O. Box 148
Mammoth Lakes, CA 93546
(619) 934-2505

Mammoth Lakes Visitor Information Center
P.O. Box 48
Mammoth Lakes, CA 93546
(619) 934-2712

Notes on the trail: From the parking area at the Shady Rest Park, retrace your path up the road. After riding .2 miles, you will arrive at a dirt road that takes off to the right (north) from the pavement. A sign reads "No Access to US 395." This dirt road is Sawmill Road. Turn right and follow Sawmill Road. Many side roads and trails branch off from the route; stay on the main road toward US 395. After pedaling for about 4 miles, and just before reaching US 395, turn left onto a dirt road. Ride parallel to the highway in a northerly direction. Follow the dirt road as it curves to the left and takes you down a steep hill. You will soon arrive at the unsigned, paved Mammoth Scenic Loop Road. Turn left and ride for 3 miles on Mammoth Scenic Loop Road and pass a small sign for Inyo Craters. Turn right just beyond the sign onto a dirt road that leads past an interpretive display. Stay on the main road and follow the signs to the Inyo Craters Trailhead. Lock your bike and hike the .2 miles to the Craters. Return the way you came to Mammoth Scenic Loop Road and turn right. Cycle about 3 miles to CA 203 and turn left toward the signed Mammoth Business District. In 1 mile turn left at a stoplight to continue on CA 203. Ride through Mammoth Lakes and turn left onto the entrance road for the Shady Rest Campground. Proceed north to your vehicle.

RIDE 50   *MINARET TRAIL*

This 4.8-mile round-trip out-and-back is a short but strenuous ride. There are some extremely steep hills where pushing your bike will be necessary. Good bike handling skills are needed on the steep and rocky descent. For the first one-half mile the riding is up and down with some easy climbing. For the next two miles you climb a series of steep hills interspersed with "rest areas." The road is rocky and rutted, but mostly in fair condition.

Although this ride is an uphill "grunt," and much of it is a hike with your bike, the views at the top are spectacular. The air and the vegetation get thinner as you climb higher along the San Joaquin Ridge. A few wind-ravaged pines cling to the hillsides, but the tree line is far below. Take a map with you to help pick out specific landmarks. Lake Crowley and the Big and Little Alkali Lakes are to the east. To the south lie Mammoth Mountain and the peaks of the John Muir Wilderness Area. Directly west are the jagged Minarets, Mt. Ritter, and the Ansel Adams Wilderness Area. To the north are June, Silver, and Grant Lakes, all glistening in the distance. While descending, look down to the southwest for lovely views of the Devil's Postpile/Reds Meadow area.

General location: The route begins near Minaret Summit in the Inyo National Forest, about 5 miles west of the town of Mammoth Lakes and approximately 40 miles north of Bishop.
Elevation change: Start the ride at 9,200′. After 1 mile of climbing you reach 9,700′. A high point of 10,250′ is reached at the turnaround point. Total elevation gain: 1,050′.
Season: Late spring through early fall. Expect sudden weather changes at any time. Carry extra clothing and a windbreaker; it is often windy and cold at the top of the ride.
Services: There is no water on this ride. All services are available in Mammoth Lakes.
Hazards: Control your speed on the steep descent; there is loose gravel, rocks, and some large ruts. Watch for hikers, cyclists, and motor vehicles.
Rescue index: Help can be found in Mammoth Lakes.
Land status: National forest.
Maps: The "Bicycle Routes—Mammoth Lakes, California" brochure/map is a good guide to this ride. It is available at the Mammoth Lakes Visitor Information

RIDE 50 *MINARET TRAIL*

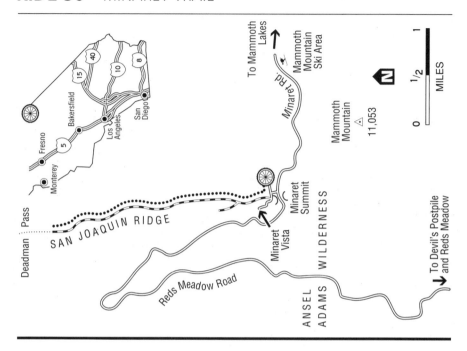

Center on Main Street (CA 203) in Mammoth Lakes. The brochure describes the trip as easy to moderately difficult; we found it to be strenuous. [This means the trail is tough, for I've ridden with Chris and Laurie and they left me in the dust.—*Editor's note.*]

Finding the trail: From US 395, take the Mammoth Lakes Exit. Follow CA 203 west for approximately 3 miles to the town of Mammoth Lakes. Continue on CA 203 (now Main Street) through town. The road name changes from Main Street to Minaret Road after a couple of miles. Follow this main road about 5 more miles, passing Mammoth Mountain Ski Area, to the road that leads to Minaret Vista Observation Point on the right (north) side of the road. Turn right toward Minaret Vista Observation Point and immediately turn right again to park in the dirt parking area.

Sources of additional information:

Inyo National Forest
Mammoth Ranger District
P.O. Box 148
Mammoth Lakes, CA 93546
(619) 934-2505

A view of the Ritter Range from the top of Minaret Trail.

Mammoth Lakes Visitor Information Center
P.O. Box 48
Mammoth Lakes, CA 93546
(619) 934-2712

Notes on the trail: From the dirt parking area, turn right onto the paved entrance road and take the second gravel road to the right. This road takes you north toward a prominent landmark—Two Teats. After approximately .5 miles, stay to the right as several trails branch off. Cross a rocky meadow in another .5 miles and continue to follow the main road. Ride 1.5 miles further to a crest near some stunted evergreens. The road deteriorates from here and is not recommended for mountain bikes. Return the way you came.

The Minaret Vista Observation Point, .3 miles north of the ride's starting point, is a nice place to enjoy the view of the Reds Meadow area and the Ritter Range. It is reached by turning right out of the recommended parking area and onto the paved road that leads to the observation point.

"Chris, darling, which way from here?"

Glossary

This short list of terms does not contain all the words used by mountain bike enthusiasts when discussing their sport. But it should be sufficient as an introduction to the lingo you'll hear on the trails.

ATB
all-terrain bike; this, like "fat-tire bike," is another name for a mountain bike

ATV
all-terrain vehicle; this usually refers to the loud, fume-spewing three- or four-wheeled motorized vehicles you will not enjoy meeting on the trail—except of course if you crash and have to hitch a ride out on one

bladed
refers to a dirt road which has been smoothed out by the use of a wide blade on earth-moving equipment; "blading" gets rid of the teeth-chattering, much-cursed washboards found on so many dirt roads after heavy vehicle use

blaze
a mark on a tree made by chipping away a piece of the bark, usually done to designate a trail; such trails are sometimes described as "blazed"

BLM
Bureau of Land Management, an agency of the federal government

buffed
used to describe a very smooth trail or an extremely fit rider

catching air
taking a jump in such a way that both wheels of the bike are off the ground at the same time

cattle guard
a set of bars placed at grade, over a depression in the road; cows find them very discouraging—their hoofs fall into the spaces between the bars

clean
while this can be used to describe what you and your bike *won't* be after following many trails, the term is most often used as a verb to denote the action of pedaling a tough section of trail successfully

deadfall
a tangled mass of fallen trees or branches

diversion ditch
a usually narrow, shallow ditch dug across or around a trail; funneling the water in this manner keeps it from destroying the trail

double-track the dual tracks made by a jeep or other vehicle, with grass or weeds or rocks between; the mountain biker can therefore ride in either of the tracks, but will of course find that whichever is chosen, no matter how many times he or she changes back and forth, the other track will appear to offer smoother travel

dugway a steep, unpaved, switchbacked descent

feathering using a light touch on the brake lever, hitting it lightly many times rather than very hard or locking the brake

four-wheel-drive this refers to any vehicle with drive-wheel capability on all four wheels (a jeep, for instance, as compared with a two-wheel-drive passenger car), or to a rough road or trail which requires four-wheel-drive capability (or a *one*-wheel-drive mountain bike!) to traverse it

game trail the usually narrow trail made by deer, elk, or other game

gated everyone knows what a gate is, and how many variations exist upon this theme; well, if a trail is described as "gated" it simply has a gate across it; don't forget that the rule is if you find a gate closed, close it behind you; if you find one open, leave it that way

Giardia shorthand for *Giardia lamblia,* and known as the "backpacker's bane" until we mountain bikers appropriated it; this is a waterborne parasite that begins its life cycle when swallowed, and one to four weeks later has its host (you) bloated, vomiting, shivering with chills and living in the bathroom; the disease can be avoided by "treating" (purifying) the water you acquire along the trail (see "Hitting the Trail")

gnarly a term thankfully used less and less these days, it refers to tough trails

hammer to ride very hard

hardpack used to describe a trail in which the dirt surface is packed down hard; such trails make for good and fast riding, and very painful landings; bikers most often use "hardpack" as both a noun and adjective, and "hard-packed" as an adjective only (the grammar lesson will help you when diagramming sentences in camp)

jeep road, jeep trail a rough road or trail which requires four-wheel-drive capability (or a horse or mountain bike) to traverse it

kamikaze	while this once referred primarily to those Japanese fliers who quaffed a glass of saki, then flew off as human bombs in suicide missions against U.S. naval vessels, it has more recently been applied to the idiot mountain bikers who, far less honorably, scream down hiking trails, endangering the physical and mental safety of the walking, biking, and equestrian traffic they meet; deck guns were necessary to stop the Japanese kamikaze pilots, but a bike pump or walking staff in the spokes is sufficient for the current-day kamikazes who threaten to get us all kicked off the trails
multi-purpose	a BLM designation of land which is open to multi-purpose use; mountain biking is allowed
out-and-back	a ride in which you will return on the same trail you pedaled out; while this might sound far more boring than a loop route, many trails look very different when pedaled in the opposite direction
portage	to carry your bike on your person
quads	bikers use this term to refer both to the extensor muscle in the front of the thigh (which is separated into four parts), and to USGS maps; the expression "Nice quads!" refers always to the former, however, except in those instances when the speaker is an engineer
runoff	rainwater or snowmelt
signed	a signed trail is denoted by signs in place of blazes
single-track	a single track through grass or brush or over rocky terrain, often created by deer, elk, or backpackers; single-track riding is some of the best fun around
slickrock	the rock-hard, compacted sandstone which is *great* to ride and even prettier to look at; you'll appreciate it more if you think of it as a petrified sand dune or seabed, and if the rider before you hasn't left tire marks (through unnecessary skidding) or granola bar wrappers behind
snowmelt	runoff produced by the melting of snow
snowpack	unmelted snow accumulated over weeks or months of winter, or over years in high-mountain terrain
spur	a road or trail which intersects the main trail you're following

tank trap	a steep-sided ditch dug across a road to restrict vehicular access
technical	terrain that is difficult to ride due not to its grade (steepness) but because of obstacles—rocks, logs, ledges, loose soil . . .
topo	short for topographical map, the kind that shows both linear distance *and* elevation gain and loss; "topo" is pronounced with both vowels long
trashed	a trail which has been destroyed (same term used no matter what has destroyed it . . . cattle, horses, or even mountain bikers riding when the ground was too wet)
two-wheel-drive	this refers to any vehicle with drive-wheel capability on only two wheels (a passenger car, for instance, compared to a jeep), or to an easy road or trail which a two-wheel-drive vehicle could traverse
water bar	earth, rock, or wooden structure which funnels water off trails
washboarded	a road with many ridges spaced closely together, like the ripples on a washboard; these make for very rough riding, and even worse driving in a car or jeep
wilderness area	land that is officially set aside by the Federal Government to remain *natural*—pure, pristine, and untrammeled by any vehicle, including mountain bikes; though mountain bikes had not been born in 1964 (when the United States Congress passed the Wilderness Act, establishing the National Wilderness Preservation system) they are considered a "form of mechanical transport" and are thereby excluded; in short, stay out
wind chill	a reference to the wind's cooling effect upon exposed flesh; for example, if the temperature is 10 degrees Fahrenheit and the wind is blowing at 20 miles per hour, the wind-chill effect (that is, the actual temperature to which your skin reacts) is *minus* 32 degrees; if you are riding in wet conditions things are even worse, for the wind-chill effect would then be *minus 74 degrees!*
windfall	anything (trees, limbs, brush, fellow bikers) blown down by the wind

LAURIE LEMAN was born in Vancouver, British Columbia. There she grew to love Elvis, ice hockey, and Canadian beer. CHRIS LEMAN grew up in Detroit, Michigan. His early youth was spent playing army, eating mud pies, and running down passersby with his tricycle. They met while working as bicycle tour leaders in Canada, and now live in Ketchum, Idaho. When not writing best-selling mountain bike guides Laurie works as a pasta slinger at a local restaurant, and helps coach the community's cross-country ski team. Chris is an apprentice carpenter and spends his free time trying to keep up with his wife on the trails.

The Mountain Bike Way to Knowledge is through William Nealy

No other great Zen master approaches William Nealy in style or originality. His handwritten text, signature cartoons, and off-beat sense of humor have made him a household name among bikers. His expertise, acquired through years of meditation (and some crash and burn), enables him to translate hard-learned reflexes and instinctive responses into his unique, easy-to-understand drawings. Anyone who wants to learn from the master (and even those who don't) will get a good laugh.

Mountain Bike!
A Manual of Beginning to Advanced Technique

The ultimate mountain bike book for the totally honed! Master the techniques of mountain biking and have a good laugh while logging miles with Nealy.

Soft cover, 172 pages, 7" by 10"
Cartoon illustrations
$12.95

The Mountain Bike Way of Knowledge

This is the first compendium of mountain bike "insider" knowledge ever published. Between the covers of this book are the secrets of wheelie turns, log jumps, bar hops, dog evasion techniques, and much more! Nealy shares his wisdom with beginner and expert alike in this self-help manual.

Soft cover, 128 pages, 8" by 5 1/2"
Cartoon illustrations
$6.95

From Menasha Ridge Press
1-800-247-9437

Out here—there's no one to ask directions

...except your **FALCON**GUIDE.

FALCONGUIDES is a series of recreation guidebooks designed to help you safely enjoy the great outdoors. Each title features up-to-date maps, photos, and detailed information on access, hazards, side trips, special attractions, and more. The 6 x 9" softcover format makes every book an ideal companion as you discover the scenic wonders around you.

FALCONGUIDES...lead the way!

Dennis Coello's America By Mountain Bike Series

Happy Trails

Hop on your mountain bike and let our guidebooks take you on America's classic trails and rides. These "where-to" books are published jointly by Falcon Press and Menasha Ridge Press and written by local biking experts. Twenty regional books will blanket the country when the series is complete.

Choose from an assortment of rides—easy rambles to all-day treks. Guides contain helpful trail and route descriptions, mountain bike shop listings, and interesting facts on area history. Each trail is described in terms of difficulty, scenery, condition, length, and elevation change. The guides also explain trail hazards, nearby services and ranger stations, how much water to bring, and what kind of gear to pack.

So before you hit the trail, grab one of our guidebooks to help make your outdoor adventures safe and memorable.

Call or write
Falcon Press or Menasha Ridge Press
Falcon Press
P.O. Box 1718, Helena, MT 59624

1-800-582-2665

Menasha Ridge Press
3169 Cahaba Heights Road, Birmingham, AL 35243
1-800-247-9437

Falcon Press

Menasha Ridge Press